GOD
DOES
CARE

GOD
DOES
CARE

Thomas Nelson Publishers

Library of Congress Cataloging-in-Publication Data

God does care.

ISBN 0-913367-00-1
1. God—Love—Biblical teaching. 2. God—Love—Prayer-
books and devotions—English. 3. Caring—Biblical teaching.
4. Caring—Religious aspects—Christianity—Prayer-books and
devotions—English. I. Word Publishing.

CONTENTS

Contents

2. We Are Commanded To Care For Those Around Us By... • 147

God Cares
Enough To...

Create Us In His Own Image

And the Lord God formed man *of* the dust of the ground, and breathed into his nostrils the breath of life; and man became a living soul.

Genesis 2:7

And God said, Let us make man in our image, after our likeness: and let them have dominion over the fish of the sea, and over the fowl of the air, and over the cattle, and over all the earth, and over every creeping thing that creepeth upon the earth.

So God created man in his *own* image, in the image of God created he him; male and female created he them.

Genesis 1:26,27

Even every one that is called by my name: for I have created him for my glory, I have formed him; yea, I have made him.

Isaiah 43:7

The first man *is* of the earth, earthy: the second man *is* the Lord from heaven.

As *is* the earthy, such *are* they also that are earthy: and as *is* the heavenly, such *are* they also that are heavenly.

And as we have borne the image of the earthy, we shall also bear the image of the heavenly.

Now this I say, brethren, that flesh and blood cannot inherit the kingdom of God; neither doth corruption inherit incorruption.

I Corinthians 15:47-50

This *is* the book of the generations of Adam. In the day that God created man, in the likeness of God made he him;

Male and female created he them; and blessed them, and called their name Adam, in the day when they were created.

Genesis 5:1,2

As for me, I will behold thy face in righteousness: I shall be satisfied, when I awake, with thy likeness.

Psalms 17:15

Thou madest him to have dominion over the works of thy hands; thou hast put all *things* under his feet:

Psalms 8:6

Lie not one to another, seeing that ye have put off the old man with his deeds;

And have put on the new *man,* which is renewed in knowledge after the image of him that created him:

Colossians 3:9,10

Let this mind be in you, which was also in Christ Jesus:

Who, being in the form of God, thought it not robbery to be equal with God:

But made himself of no reputation, and took upon him the form of a servant, and was made in the likeness of men:

Phillippians 2:5-7

For we are his workmanship, created in Christ Jesus unto good works, which God hath before ordained that we should walk in them.

Ephesians 2:10

For a man indeed ought not to cover *his* head, forasmuch as he is the image and glory of God: but the woman is the glory of the man.

I Corinthians 11:7

For whom he did foreknow, he also did predestinate *to be* conformed to the image of his Son, that he might be the firstborn among many brethren.

Romans 8:29

Now the Lord is that Spirit: and where the Spirit of the Lord *is,* there *is* liberty.

But we all, with open face beholding as in a glass the glory of the Lord, are changed into the same image from glory to glory, *even* as by the Spirit of the Lord.

II Corinthians 3:17,18

Beloved, now are we the sons of God, and it doth not yet appear what we shall be: but we know that, when he shall appear, we shall be like him; for we shall see him as he is.

I John 3:2

Call Us His Children

And because ye are sons, God hath sent forth the Spirit of his Son into your hearts, crying, Abba, Father.

Wherefore thou art no more a servant, but a son; and if a son, then an heir of God through Christ.

Galatians 4:6,7

For ye are all the children of God by faith in Christ Jesus.

Galatians 3:26

Or what man is there of you, whom if his son ask bread, will he give him a stone?

Or if he ask a fish, will he give him a serpent?

If ye then, being evil, know how to give good gifts unto your children, how much more shall your Father which is in heaven give good things to them that ask him?

Matthew 7:9-11

And he said unto me, It is done. I am Alpha and Omega, the beginning and the end. I will give unto him that is athirst of the fountain of the water of life freely.

He that overcometh shall inherit all things; and I will be his God, and he shall be my son.

Revelation 21:6,7

Wherefore come out from among them, and be ye separate, saith the Lord, and touch not the unclean *thing*; and I will receive you.

And will be a Father unto you, and ye shall be my sons and daughters, saith the Lord Almighty.

II Corinthians 6:17,18

For ye have not received the spirit of bondage again to fear; but ye have received the Spirit of adoption, whereby we cry, Abba, Father.

The Spirit itself beareth witness with our spirit, that we are the children of God:

And if children, then heirs; heirs of God, and joint-heirs with Christ; if so be that we suffer with *him,* that we may be also glorified together.

Romans 8:15-17

But as many as received him, to them gave he power to become the sons of God, *even* to them that believe on his name.

John 1:12

Beloved, now are we the sons of God, and it doth not yet appear what we shall be: but we know that, when he shall appear, we shall be like him; for we shall see him as he is.

I John 3:2

Make Us His People

For this *is* the covenant that I will make with the house of Israel after those days, saith the Lord; I will put my laws into their mind, and write them in their hearts: and I will be to them a God, and they shall be to me a people:

Hebrews 8:10

This people have I formed for myself; they shall shew forth my praise.

Isaiah 43:21

For we are his workmanship, created in Christ Jesus unto good works, which God hath before ordained that we should walk in them.

Ephesians 2:10

And what agreement hath the temple of God with idols? for ye are the temple of the living God; as God hath said, I will dwell in them, and walk in *them;* and I will be their God, and they shall be my people.

II Corinthians 6:16

The Lord will give strength unto his people; the Lord will bless his people with peace.

Psalms 29:11

And I will make of thee a great nation, and I will bless thee, and make thy name great; and thou shalt be a blessing:

Genesis 12:2

But now thus saith the Lord that created thee, O Jacob, and he that formed thee, O Israel, Fear not: for I have redeemed thee, I have called *thee* by thy name; thou *art* mine.

When thou passest through the waters, I *will be* with thee; and through the rivers, they shall not overflow thee: when thou walkest through the fire, thou shalt not be burned; neither shall the flame kindle upon thee.

For I *am* the Lord thy God, the Holy One of Israel, thy Saviour: I gave Egypt *for* thy ransom, Ethiopia and Seba for thee.

Isaiah 43:1-3

I will hear what God the Lord will speak: for he will speak peace unto his people, and to his saints: but let them not turn again to folly.

Psalms 85:8

Being confident of this very thing, that he which hath begun a good work in you will perform *it* until the day of Jesus Christ:

Philippians 1:6

But we all, with open face beholding as in a glass the glory of the Lord, are changed into the same image from glory to glory, *even* as by the Spirit of the Lord.

II Corinthians 3:18

For we are labourers together with God: ye are God's husbandry, *ye are* God's building.

I Corinthians 3:9

As he saith also in Osee, I will call them my people, which were not my people; and her beloved, which was not beloved.

And it shall come to pass, *that* in the place where it was said unto them, Ye *are* not my people; there shall they be be called the children of the living God.

Romans 9:25,26

The Lord shall increase you more and more, you and your children.

Psalms 115:14

House and riches *are* the inheritance of fathers: and a prudent wife *is* from the Lord.

Proverbs 19:14

Give Us New Life

But whosoever drinketh of the water that I shall give him shall never thirst; but the water that I shall give him shall be in him a well of water springing up into everlasting life.

John 4:14

Blessed *are* they that do his commandments, that they may have right to the tree of life, and may enter in through the gates into the city.

Revelation 22:14

Blessed *be* the God and Father of our Lord Jesus Christ, which according to his abundant mercy hath begotten us again unto a lively hope by the resurrection of Jesus Christ from the dead,

To an inheritance incorruptible, and undefiled, and that fadeth not away, reserved in heaven for you,

I Peter 1:3,4

He that hath the Son hath life; *and* he that hath not the Son of God hath not life.

I John 5:12

It is a faithful saying: For if we be dead with *him,* we shall also live with *him*:
II Timothy 2:11

Therefore if any man *be* in Christ, *he is* a new creature: old things are passed away; behold, all things are become new.
II Corinthians 5:17

For to be carnally minded *is* death; but to be spiritually minded *is* life and peace.
Romans 8:6

For if, when we were enemies, we were reconciled to God by the death of his Son, much more, being reconciled, we shall be saved by his life.
Romans 5:10

For if by one man's offence death reigned by one; much more they which receive abundance of grace and of the gift of righteousness shall reign in life by one, Jesus Christ.
Romans 5:17

Jesus said unto her, I am the resurrection, and the life: he that believeth in me, though he were dead, yet shall he live:

And whosoever liveth and believeth in me shall never die. Believest thou this?
John 11:25,26

The thief cometh not, but for to steal, and to kill, and to destroy: I am come that they might have life, and that they might have *it* more abundantly.

John 10:10

For the bread of God is he which cometh down from heaven, and giveth life unto the world.

Then said they unto him, Lord, evermore give us this bread.

And Jesus said unto them, I am the bread of life: he that cometh to me shall never hunger; and he that believeth on me shall never thirst.

John 6:33-35

Verily, verily, I say unto you, He that believeth on me hath everlasting life.

John 6:47

For by grace are ye saved through faith; and that not of yourselves: *it is* the gift of God:

Not of works, lest any man should boast.

For we are his workmanship, created in Christ Jesus unto good works, which God hath before ordained that we should walk in them.

Wherefore remember, that ye *being* in time past Gentiles in the flesh, who are called Uncircumcision by that which is called the Circumcision in the flesh made by hands;

That at that time ye were without Christ, being aliens from the commonwealth of Israel, and strangers from the covenants of promise, having no hope, and without God in the world:

But now in Christ Jesus ye who sometimes were far off are made nigh by the blood of Christ.

Ephesians 2:8-13

Raise Us From The Dead

Jesus said unto her, I am the resurrection, and the life: he that believeth in me, though he were dead, yet shall he live:

John 11:25

And this is the Father's will which hath sent me, that of all which he hath given me I should lose nothing, but should raise it up again at the last day.

And this is the will of him that sent me, that every one which seeth the Son, and believeth on him, may have everlasting life: and I will raise him up at the last day.

John 6:39,40

For if we believe that Jesus died and rose again, even so them also which sleep in Jesus will God bring with him.

I Thessalonians 4:14

Then we which are alive *and* remain shall be caught up together with them in the clouds, to meet the Lord in the air: and so shall we ever be with the Lord.

I Thessalonians 4:17

Yet a little while, and the world seeth me no more; but ye see me: because I live, ye shall live also.

John 14:19

But if the Spirit of him that raised up Jesus from the dead dwell in you, he that raised up Christ from the dead shall also quicken your mortal bodies by his Spirit that dwelleth in you.

Romans 8:11

He that findeth his life shall lose it: and he that loseth his life for my sake shall find it.
Matthew 10:39

For to me to live *is* Christ, and to die *is* gain.

Phillippians 1:21

And you *hath he quickened,* who were dead in trespasses and sins;
Ephesians 2:1

And hath raised *us* up together, and made *us* sit together in heavenly *places* in Christ Jesus:
Ephesians 2:6

We having the same spirit of faith, according as it is written, I believed, and therefore have I spoken; we also believe, and therefore speak;
Knowing that he which raised up the Lord Jesus shall raise up us also by Jesus, and shall present *us* with you.
II Corinthians 4:13,14

And as we have borne the image of the earthy, we shall also bear the image of the heavenly.

I Corinthians 15:49

Behold, I shew you a mystery; We shall not all sleep, but we shall all be changed,

I Corinthians 15:51

In a moment, in the twinkling of an eye, at the last trump: for the trumpet shall sound, and the dead shall be raised incorruptible, and we shall be changed.

I Corinthians 15:52

So when this corruptible shall have put on incorruption, and this mortal shall have put on immortality, then shall be brought to pass the saying that is written, Death is swallowed up in victory.

O death, where *is* thy sting? O grave, where *is* thy victory?

The sting of death *is* sin; and the strength of sin *is* the law.

But thanks *be* to God, which giveth us the victory through our Lord Jesus Christ.

Therefore, my beloved brethren, be ye stedfast, unmoveable, always abounding in the work of the Lord, forasmuch as ye know that your labour is not in vain in the Lord.

I Corinthians 15:54-58

For since by man *came* death, by man *came* also the resurrection of the dead.

For as in Adam all die, even so in Christ shall all be made alive.

I Corinthians 15:21,22

Marvel not at this: for the hour is coming, in the which all that are in the graves shall hear his voice,

And shall come forth; they that have done good, unto the resurrection of life; and they that have done evil, unto the resurrection of damnation.

John 5:28,29

He will swallow up death in victory; and the Lord God will wipe away tears from off all faces; and the rebuke of his people shall he take away from off all the earth: for the Lord hath spoken *it*.

Isaiah 25:8

Give Us Eternal Life

Let not your heart be troubled: ye believe in God, believe also in me.

In my Father's house are many mansions: if *it were* not *so*, I would have told you. I go to prepare a place for you.

And if I go and prepare a place for you, I will come again, and receive you unto myself; that where I am, *there* ye may be also.

John 14:1-3

My sheep hear my voice, and I know them, and they follow me:

And I give unto them eternal life; and they shall never perish, neither shall any *man* pluck them out of my hand.

John 10:27,28

And this is the Father's will which hath sent me, that of all which he hath given me I should lose nothing, but should raise it up again at the last day.

John 6:39

But God will redeem my soul from the power of the grave: for he shall receive me. Selah.

Psalms 49:15

To him that overcometh will I grant to sit with me in my throne, even as I also overcame, and am set down with my Father in his throne.

Revelation 3:21

And this is the record, that God hath given to us eternal life, and this life is in his Son.

He that hath the Son hath life; *and* he that hath not the Son of God hath not life.

I John 5:11,12

And there shall be no night there; and they need no candle, neither light of the sun; for the Lord God giveth them light: and they shall reign for ever and ever.

Revelation 22:5

For we know that if our earthly house of *this* tabernacle were dissolved, we have a building of God, an house not made with hands, eternal in the heavens.

II Corinthians 5:1

And I appoint unto you a kingdom, as my Father hath appointed unto me;

That ye may eat and drink at my table in my kingdom, and sit on thrones judging the twelve tribes of Israel.

Luke 22:29,30

Fear not, little flock; for it is your Father's good pleasure to give you the kingdom.

Luke 12:32

For God so loved the world, that he gave his only begotten Son, that whosoever believeth in him should not perish, but have everlasting life.

John 3:16

He that loveth his life shall lose it; and he that hateth his life in this world shall keep it unto life eternal.

John 12:25

Verily, verily, I say unto you, He that believeth on me hath everlasting life.

John 6:47

Verily, verily, I say unto you, He that heareth my word, and believeth on him that sent me, hath everlasting life, and shall not come into condemnation; but is passed from death unto life.

John 5:24

Love Us Unconditionally

But God, who is rich in mercy, for his great love wherewith he loved us,

Even when we were dead in sins, hath quickened us together with Christ, *by grace ye are saved;*

Ephesians 2:4,5

That Christ may dwell in your hearts by faith; that ye, being rooted and grounded in love,

May be able to comprehend with all saints what *is* the breadth, and length, and depth, and height;

And to know the love of Christ, which passeth knowledge, that ye might be filled with all the fulness of God.

Ephesians 3:17-19

Herein is love, not that we loved God, but that he loved us, and sent his Son *to be* the propitiation for our sins.

I John 4:10

And we have known and believed the love that God hath to us. God is love; and he that dwelleth in love dwelleth in God, and God in him.

I John 4:16

Who shall separate us from the love of Christ? *shall* tribulation, or distress, or persecution, or famine, or nakedness, or peril, or sword?

Romans 8:35

For I am persuaded, that neither death, nor life, nor angels, nor principalities, nor powers, nor things present, nor things to come,

Nor height, nor depth, nor any other creature, shall be able to separate us from the love of God, which is in Christ Jesus our Lord.

Romans 8:38,39

And hope maketh not ashamed; because the love of God is shed abroad in our hearts by the Holy Ghost which is given unto us.

For when we were yet without strength, in due time Christ died for the ungodly.

For scarcely for a righteous man will one die: yet peradventure for a good man some would even dare to die.

But God commendeth his love toward us, in that, while we were yet sinners, Christ died for us.

Romans 5:5-8

Likewise, I say unto you, there is joy in the presence of the angels of God over one sinner that repenteth.

Luke 15:10

The Lord hath appeared of old unto me, *saying,* Yea, I have loved thee with an everlasting love: therefore with lovingkindness have I drawn thee.

Jeremiah 31:3

Surely he hath borne our griefs, and carried our sorrows: yet we did esteem him stricken, smitten of God, and afflicted.

But he *was* wounded for our transgressions, *he was* bruised for our iniquities: the chastisement of our peace *was* upon him; and with his stripes we are healed.

All we like sheep have gone astray; we have turned every one to his own way; and the Lord hath laid on him the iniquity of us all.

Isaiah 53:4-6

This *is* a faithful saying, and worthy of all acceptation, that Christ Jesus came into the world to save sinners; of whom I am chief.

I Timothy 1:15

According as he hath chosen us in him before the foundation of the world, that we should be holy and without blame before him in love:

Having predestinated us unto the adoption of children by Jesus Christ to himself, according to the good pleasure of his will,

To the praise of the glory of his grace, wherein he hath made us accepted in the beloved.

Ephesians 1:4-6

He that spared not his own Son, but delivered him up for us all, how shall he not with him also freely give us all things?

Romans 8:32

Fill Us With His Spirit

And I will pray the Father, and he shall give you another Comforter, that he may abide with you for ever;

Even the Spirit of truth; whom the world cannot receive, because it seeth him not, neither knoweth him: but ye know him; for he dwelleth with you, and shall be in you.

John 14:16,17

But the Comforter, *which is* the Holy Ghost, whom the Father will send in my name, he shall teach you all things, and bring all things to your remembrance, whatsoever I have said unto you.

John 14:26

Then Peter said unto them, Repent, and be baptized every one of you in the name of Jesus Christ for the remission of sins, and ye shall receive the gift of the Holy Ghost.

Acts 2:38

Hereby know we that we dwell in him, and he in us, because he hath given us of his Spirit.

I John 4:13

For our gospel came not unto you in word only, but also in power, and in the Holy Ghost, and in much assurance; as ye know what manner of men we were among you for your sake.

And ye became followers of us, and of the Lord, having received the word in much affliction, with joy of the Holy Ghost:

I Thessalonians 1:5,6

But God hath revealed *them* unto us by his Spirit: for the Spirit searcheth all things, yea, the deep things of God.

I Corinthians 2:10

Now the God of hope fill you with all joy and peace in believing, that ye may abound in hope, through the power of the Holy Ghost.

Romans 15:13

And they were all filled with the Holy Ghost, and began to speak with other tongues, as the Spirit gave them utterance.

Acts 2:4

But when the Comforter is come, whom I will send unto you from the Father, *even* the Spirit of truth, which proceedeth from the Father, he shall testify of me;

John 15:26

It is the spirit that quickeneth; the flesh profiteth nothing: the words that I speak unto you, *they* are spirit, and *they* are life.

John 6:63

Give Us Spiritual Gifts

But unto every one of us is given grace according to the measure of the gift of Christ.

Wherefore he saith, When he ascended up on high, he led captivity captive, and gave gifts unto men.

Ephesians 4:7,8

Now there are diversities of gifts, but the same Spirit.

And there are differences of administrations, but the same Lord.

And there are diversities of operations, but it is the same God which worketh all in all.

But the manifestation of the Spirit is given to every man to profit withal.

For to one is given by the Spirit the word of wisdom; to another the word of knowledge by the same Spirit;

To another faith by the same Spirit; to another the gifts of healing by the same Spirit;

To another the working of miracles; to another prophecy; to another discerning of spirits; to another *divers* kinds of tongues; to another the interpretation of tongues:

But all these worketh that one and the selfsame Spirit, dividing to every man severally as he will.

For as the body is one, and hath many members, and all the members of that one body, being many, are one body: so also *is* Christ.

I Corinthians 12:4-12

Neglect not the gift that is in thee, which was given thee by prophecy, with the laying on of the hands of the presbytery.

I Timothy 4:14

And it shall come to pass afterward, *that* I will pour out my spirit upon all flesh; and your sons and your daughters shall prophesy, your old men shall dream dreams, your young men shall see visions:

Joel 2:28

As every man hath received the gift, *even so* minister the same one to another, as good stewards of the manifold grace of God.

I Peter 4:10

Every good gift and every perfect gift is from above, and cometh down from the Father of lights, with whom is no variableness, neither shadow of turning.

James 1:17

Whereof I was made a minister, according to the gift of the grace of God given unto me by the effectual working of his power.

Ephesians 3:7

Blessed *be* the God and Father of our Lord Jesus Christ, who hath blessed us with all spiritual blessings in heavenly *places* in Christ:

Ephesians 1:3

For I would that all men were even as I myself. But every man hath his proper gift of God, one after this manner, and another after that.

I Corinthians 7:7

For as we have many members in one body, and all members have not the same office:

So we, *being* many, are one body in Christ, and every one members one of another.

Having then gifts differing according to the grace that is given to us, whether prophecy, *let us prophesy* according to the proportion of faith;

Or ministry, *let us wait* on *our* ministering: or he that teacheth, on teaching;

Or he that exhorteth, on exhortation: he that giveth, *let him do it* with simplicity; he that ruleth, with diligence; he that sheweth mercy, with cheerfulness.

Romans 12:4-8

For God is my witness, whom I serve with my spirit in the gospel of his Son, that without ceasing I make mention of you always in my prayers;

Making request, if by any means now at length I might have a prosperous journey by the will of God to come unto you.

For I long to see you, that I may impart unto you some spiritual gift, to the end ye may be established;

Romans 1:9-11

Then Peter said unto them, Repent, and be baptized every one of you in the name of Jesus Christ for the remission of sins, and ye shall receive the gift of the Holy Ghost.

For the promise is unto you, and to your children, and to all that are afar off, *even* as many as the Lord our God shall call.

Acts 2:38,39

And he gave some, apostles; and some, prophets; and some, evangelists; and some, pastors and teachers;

For the perfecting of the saints, for the work of the ministry, for the edifying of the body of Christ:

Till we all come in the unity of the faith, and of the knowledge of the Son of God, unto a perfect man, unto the measure of the stature of the fulness of Christ:

Ephesians 4:11-13

Give Us Power To Witness

And Jesus came and spake unto them, saying, All power is given unto me in heaven and in earth.

Go ye therefore, and teach all nations, baptizing them in the name of the Father, and of the Son, and of the Holy Ghost:

Teaching them to observe all things whatsoever I have commanded you: and, lo, I am with you alway, *even* unto the end of the world. Amen.

Matthew 28:18-20

But when he saw the multitudes, he was moved with compassion on them, because they fainted, and were scattered abroad, as sheep having no shepherd.

Then saith he unto his disciples, The harvest truly *is* plenteous, but the labourers *are* few;

Pray ye therefore the Lord of the harvest, that he will send forth labourers into his harvest.

Matthew 9:36-38

And he saith unto them, Follow me, and I will make you fishers of men.

Matthew 4:19

Let him know, that he which converteth the sinner from the error of his way shall
save a soul from death, and shall hide a multitude of sins.

James 5:20

Now therefore go, and I will be with
thy mouth, and teach thee what thou shalt
say.

Exodus 4:12

But they that wait upon the Lord shall
renew *their* strength; they shall mount up
with wings as eagles; they shall run, and not
be weary; *and* they shall walk, and not faint.

Isaiah 40:31

The fruit of the righteous *is* a tree of
life; and he that winneth souls *is* wise.

Proverbs 11:30

Withal praying also for us, that God
would open unto us a door of utterance, to
speak the mystery of Christ, for which I am
also in bonds:
That I may make it manifest, as I ought
to speak.

Colossians 4:3,4

That he would grant you, according to
the riches of his glory, to be strengthened
with might by his Spirit in the inner man;

Ephesians 3:16

Now unto him that is able to do exceeding abundantly above all that we ask or think, according to the power that worketh in us,

Unto him *be* glory in the church by Christ Jesus throughout all ages, world without end. Amen.

Ephesians 3:20-21

To another faith by the same Spirit; to another the gifts of healing by the same Spirit;

I Corinthians 12:9

And now, Lord, behold their threatenings: and grant unto thy servants, that with all boldness they may speak thy word,

Acts 4:29

But ye shall receive power, after that the Holy Ghost is come upon you: and ye shall be witnesses unto me both in Jerusalem, and in all Judaea, and in Samaria, and unto the uttermost part of the earth.

Acts 1:8

For the Holy Ghost shall teach you in the same hour what ye ought to say.

Luke 12:12

Give Us His Word

As newborn babes, desire the sincere milk of the word, that ye may grow thereby:

I Peter 2:2

Heaven and earth shall pass away, but my words shall not pass away.

Matthew 24:35

For verily I say unto you, Till heaven and earth pass, one jot or one tittle shall in no wise pass from the law, till all be fulfilled.

Matthew 5:18

But the word of the Lord endureth for ever. And this is the word which by the gospel is preached unto you.

I Peter 1:25

The law of the Lord *is* perfect, converting the soul: the testimony of the *Lord* is sure, making wise the simple.

The statutes of the Lord *are* right, rejoicing the heart: the commandment of the Lord *is* pure, enlightening the eyes.

Psalms 19:7,8

And he humbled thee, and suffered thee to hunger, and fed thee with manna, which thou knewest not, neither did thy fathers know; that he might make thee know that man doth not live by bread only, but by every *word* that proceedeth out of the mouth of the Lord doth man live.

Deuteronomy 8:3

Thy words were found, and I did eat them; and thy word was unto me the joy and rejoicing of mine heart: for I am called by thy name, O Lord God of hosts.

Jeremiah 15:16

So shall my word be that goeth forth out of my mouth: it shall not return unto me void, but it shall accomplish that which I please, and it shall prosper *in the thing* whereto I sent it.

Isaiah 55:11

The grass withereth, the flower fadeth: but the word of our God shall stand for ever.

Isaiah 40:8

This *is* my comfort in my affliction: for thy word hath quickened me.

Psalms 119:50

Thy word have I hid in mine heart, that I might not sin against thee.

Psalms 119:11

For the word of God *is* quick, and powerful, and sharper than any twoedged sword, piercing even to the dividing asunder of soul and spirit, and of the joints and marrow, and *is* a discerner of the thoughts and intents of the heart.

Hebrews 4:12

So then faith *cometh* by hearing, and hearing by the word of God.

Romans 10:17

For whatsoever things were written aforetime were written for our learning, that we through patience and comfort of the scriptures might have hope.

Romans 15:4

Verily, verily, I say unto you, He that heareth my word, and believeth on him that sent me, hath everlasting life, and shall not come into condemnation; but is passed from death unto life.

John 5:24

Search the scriptures; for in them ye think ye have eternal life: and they are they which testify of me.

John 5:39

And that from a child thou hast known the holy scriptures, which are able to make thee wise unto salvation through faith which is in Christ Jesus.

All scripture *is* given by inspiration of God, and *is* profitable for doctrine, for reproof, for correction, for instruction in righteousness:

That the man of God may be perfect, throughly furnished unto all good works.

II Timothy 3:15-17

Blessed *is* he that readeth, and they that hear the words of this prophecy, and keep those things which are written therein: for the time *is* at hand.

Revelation 1:3

Search the scriptures; for in them ye think ye have eternal life: and they are they which testify of me.

John 5:39

The words of the Lord *are* pure words: *as* silver tried in a furnace of earth, purified seven times.

Thou shalt keep them, O Lord, thou shalt preserve them from this generation for ever.

Psalms 12:6,7

In the beginning was the Word, and the Word was with God, and the Word was God.

The same was in the beginning with God.

All things were made by him; and without him was not any thing made that was made.

In him was life; and the life was the light of men.

John 1:1-4

He sent his word, and healed them, and delivered *them* from their destructions.

Oh that *men* would praise the Lord *for* his goodness, and *for* his wonderful works to the children of men!

Psalms 107:20,21

Give Us Freedom Of Choice

And if it seem evil unto you to serve the Lord, choose you this day whom ye will serve; whether the gods which your fathers served that *were* on the other side of the flood, or the gods of the Amorites, in whose land ye dwell: but as for me and my house, we will serve the Lord.

Joshua 24:15

See, I have set before thee this day life and good, and death and evil;

In that I command thee this day to love the Lord thy God, to walk in his ways, and to keep his commandments and his statutes and his judgments, that thou mayest live and multiply: and the Lord thy God shall bless thee in the land whither thou goest to possess it.

But if thine heart turn away, so that thou wilt not hear, but shalt be drawn away, and worship other gods, and serve them;

I denounce unto you this day, that ye shall surely perish, *and that* ye shall not prolong *your* days upon the land, whither thou passest over Jordan to go to possess it.

I call heaven and earth to record this day against you, *that* I have set before you life and death, blessing and cursing: therefore choose life, that both thou and thy seed may live:

That thou mayest love the Lord thy God, *and* that thou mayest obey his voice, and that thou mayest cleave unto him: for he *is* thy life, and the length of thy days: that thou mayest dwell in the land which the Lord sware unto thy fathers, to Abraham, to Isaac, and to Jacob, to give them.

Deuteronomy 30:15-20

For where your treasure is, there will your heart be also.

The light of the body is the eye: if therefore thine eye be single, thy whole body shall be full of light.

But if thine eye be evil, thy whole body shall be full of darkness. If therefore the light that is in thee be darkness, how great *is* that darkness!

No man can serve two masters: for either he will hate the one, and love the other; or else he will hold to the one, and despise the other. Ye cannot serve God and mammon.

Matthew 6:21-24

Even a child is known by his doings, whether his work *be* pure, and whether *it be* right.

Proverbs 20:11

A good man out of the good treasure of the heart bringeth forth good things: and an evil man out of the evil treasure bringeth forth evil things.

Matthew 12:35

Therefore to him that knoweth to do good, and doeth *it* not, to him it is sin.

James 4:17

Depart from evil, and do good; seek peace, and pursue it.

Psalms 34:14

What man *is* he that feareth the Lord? him shall he teach in the way *that* he shall choose.

Psalms 25:12

Moreover as for me, God forbid that I should sin against the Lord in ceasing to pray for you: but I will teach you the good and the right way:

I Samuel 12:23

He that walketh with wise *men* shall be wise: but a companion of fools shall be destroyed.

Proverbs 13:20

Therefore seeing we have this ministry, as we have received mercy, we faint not;

But have renounced the hidden things of dishonesty, not walking in craftiness, nor handling the word of God deceitfully; but by manifestation of the truth commending ourselves to every man's conscience in the sight of God.

II Corinthians 4:1,2

For to be carnally minded *is* death; but to be spiritually minded *is* life and peace.

Romans 8:6

Ye adulterers and adulteresses, know ye not that the friendship of the world is enmity with God? whosoever therefore will be a friend of the world is the enemy of God.

James 4:4

Speak not evil one of another, brethren. He that speaketh evil of *his* brother, and judgeth his brother, speaketh evil of the law, and judgeth the law: but if thou judge the law, thou art not a doer of the law, but a judge.

There is one lawgiver, who is able to save and to destroy: who art thou that judgest another?

James 4:11,12

Judge Us With Fairness

The fear of the Lord *is* clean, enduring for ever: the judgments of the Lord *are* true *and* righteous altogether.

More to be desired *are they* than gold, yea, than much fine gold: sweeter also than honey and the honeycomb.

Moreover by them is thy servant warned: *and* in keeping of them *there* is great reward.

Psalms 19:9-11

But the Lord shall endure for ever: he hath prepared his throne for judgment.

And he shall judge the world in righteousness, he shall minister judgment to the people in uprightness.

The Lord also will be a refuge for the oppressed, a refuge in times of trouble.

And they that know thy name will put their trust in thee: for thou, Lord, hast not forsaken them that seek thee.

Psalms 9:7-10

Let the people praise thee, O God; let all the people praise thee.

O let the nations be glad and sing for joy: for thou shalt judge the people righteously, and govern the nations upon earth. Selah.

Psalms 67:3-4

But I say unto you, That every idle word that men shall speak, they shall give account thereof in the day of judgment.

Matthew 12:36

I said in mine heart, God shall judge the righteous and the wicked: for *there is* a time there for every purpose and for every work.

Ecclesiastes 3:17

For the Lord loveth judgment, and forsaketh not his saints; they are preserved for ever: but the seed of the wicked shall be cut off.

Psalm 37:28

The Lord executeth righteousness and judgment for all that are oppressed.

Psalm 103:6

Say among the heathen *that* the Lord reigneth: the world also shall be established that it shall not be moved: he shall judge the people righteously.

Psalm 96:10

But God *is* the judge: he putteth down one, and setteth up another.

Psalm 75:7

So that a man shall say, Verily *there is* a reward for the righteous: verily he is a God that judgeth in the earth.

Psalm 58:11

But the heavens and the earth, which are now, by the same word are kept in store, reserved unto fire against the day of judgment and perdition of ungodly men.

II Peter 3:7

Therefore judge nothing before the time, until the Lord come, who both will bring to light the hidden things of darkness, and will make manifest the counsels of the hearts: and then shall every man have praise of God.

I Corinthians 4:5

But why dost thou judge thy brother? or why dost thou set at nought thy brother? for we shall all stand before the judgment seat of Christ.

Romans 14:10

Therefore thou art inexcusable, O man, whosoever thou art that judgest: for wherein thou judgest another, thou condemnest thyself; for thou that judgest doest the same things.

But we are sure that the judgment of God is according to truth against them which commit such things.

And thinkest thou this, O man, that judgest them which do such things, and doest the same, that thou shalt escape the judgment of God?

Or despisest thou the riches of his goodness and forbearance and longsuffering; not knowing that the goodness of God leadeth thee to repentance?

But after thy hardness and impenitent heart treasurest up unto thyself wrath against the day of wrath and revelation of the righteous judgment of God;

Who will render to every man according to his deeds:

Romans 2:1-6

In the day when God shall judge the secrets of men by Jesus Christ according to my gospel.

Romans 2:16

Deliver Us From Temptation

There hath no temptation taken you but such as is common to man: but God *is* faithful, who will not suffer you to be tempted above that ye are able; but will with the temptation also make a way to escape, that ye may be able to bear *it*.

I Corinthians 10:13

Because thou has kept the word of my patience, I also will keep thee from the hour of temptation, which shall come upon all the world, to try them that dwell upon the earth.

Revelation 3:10

The Lord knoweth how to deliver the godly out of temptations, and to reserve the unjust unto the day of judgment to be punished:

II Peter 2:9

Wherefore take unto you the whole armour of God, that ye may be able to withstand in the evil day, and having done all, to stand.

Stand therefore, having your loins girt about with truth, and having on the breastplate of righteousness;

And your feet shod with the preparation of the gospel of peace;

Above all, taking the shield of faith, wherewith ye shall be able to quench all the fiery darts of the wicked.

And take the helmet of salvation, and the sword of the Spirit, which is the word of God:

Ephesians 6:13-17

For we have not an high priest which cannot be touched with the feeling of our infirmities; but was in all points tempted like as *we are, yet* without sin.

Hebrews 4:15

For in that he himself hath suffered being tempted, he is able to succour them that are tempted.

Hebrews 2:18

Nay, in all these things we are more than conquerors through him that loved us.

Romans 8:37

I pray not that thou shouldest take them out of the world, but that thou shouldest keep them from the evil.

John 17:15

Cast thy burden upon the Lord, and he shall sustain thee: he shall never suffer the righteous to be moved.

Psalm 55:22

Surely he shall deliver thee from the snare of the fowler, *and* from the noisome pestilence.

He shall cover thee with his feathers, and under his wings shalt thou trust: his truth *shall be thy* shield and buckler.

Psalm 91:3,4

And the Lord shall deliver me from every evil work, and will preserve *me* unto his heavenly kingdom: to whom *be* glory for ever and ever. Amen.

II Timothy 4:18

But the Lord is faithful, who shall stablish you, and keep *you* from evil.

II Thessalonians 3:3

The Lord shall preserve thee from all evil: he shall preserve thy soul.

The Lord shall preserve thy going out and thy coming in from this time forth, and even for evermore.

Psalm 121:7,8

He will not suffer thy foot to be moved: he that keepeth thee will not slumber.

Psalm 121:3

Hold up my goings in thy paths, *that* my footsteps slip not.

I have called upon thee, for thou wilt hear me, O God: incline thine ear unto me, *and hear* my speech.

Shew thy marvellous lovingkindness, O thou that savest by thy right hand them which put their trust *in thee* from those that rise up *against them.*

Keep me as the apple of the eye, hide me under the shadow of thy wings,

Psalm 17:5-8

Save Us From Our Sins

To him give all the prophets witness, that through his name whosoever believeth in him shall receive remission of sins.

Acts 10:43

Who his own self bare our sins in his own body on the tree, that we, being dead to sins, should live unto righteousness: by whose stripes ye were healed.

I Peter 2:24

Blessed *is he whose* transgression *is* forgiven, *whose* sin *is* covered.
Blessed *is* the man unto whom the Lord imputeth not iniquity, and in whose spirit *there is* no guile.

Psalm 32:1,2

Bless the Lord, O my soul, and forget not all his benefits:
Who forgiveth all thine iniquities; who healeth all thy diseases;

Psalm 103:2,3

My little children, these things write I unto you, that ye sin not. And if any man sin, we have an advocate with the Father, Jesus Christ the righteous:

I John 2:1

If we confess our sins, he is faithful and just to forgive us *our* sins, and to cleanse us from all unrighteousness.

I John 1:9

Wherefore he is able also to save them to the uttermost that come unto God by him, seeing he ever liveth to make intercession for them.

Hebrews 7:25

For this *is* good and acceptable in the sight of God our Saviour;
Who will have all men to be saved, and to come unto the knowledge of the truth.

I Timothy 2:3,4

And such were some of you: but ye are washed, but ye are sanctified, but ye are justified in the name of the Lord Jesus, and by the Spirit of our God.

I Corinthians 6:11

For I am not ashamed of the gospel of Christ: for it is the power of God unto salvation to every one that believeth; to the Jew first, and also to the Greek.

Romans 1:16

And they said, Believe on the Lord Jesus Christ, and thou shalt be saved, and thy house.

Acts 16:31

All that the Father giveth me shall come to me; and him that cometh to me I will in no wise cast out.

John 6:37

I have blotted out, as a thick cloud, thy transgressions, and, as a cloud, thy sins: return unto me; for I have redeemed thee.

Isaiah 44:22

I, *even* I, *am* he that blotteth out thy transgressions for mine own sake, and will not remember thy sins.

Isaiah 43:25

Come now, and let us reason together, saith the Lord: though your sins be as scarlet, they shall be as white as snow; though they be red like crimson, they shall be as wool.

Isaiah 1:18

But if we walk in the light, as he is in the light, we have fellowship one with another, and the blood of Jesus Christ his Son cleanseth us from all sin.

If we say that we have no sin, we deceive ourselves, and the truth is not in us.

If we confess our sins, he is faithful and just to forgive us *our* sins, and to cleanse us from all unrighteousness.

I John 1:7-9

In whom we have redemption through his blood, the forgiveness of sins, according to the riches of his grace;

Ephesians 1:7

For he hath made him *to be* sin for us, who knew no sin; that we might be made the righteousness of God in him.

II Corinthians 5:21

There is therefore now no condemnation to them which are in Christ Jesus, who walk not after the flesh, but after the Spirit.

For the law of the Spirit of life in Christ Jesus hath made me free from the law of sin and death.

Romans 8:1,2

And ye shall know the truth, and the truth shall make you free.

John 8:32

If the Son therefore shall make you free, ye shall be free indeed.

John 8:36

Forgive Us
When We Repent

For if I have boasted any thing to him of you, I am not ashamed; but as we spake all things to you in truth, even so our boasting, which *I made* before Titus, is found a truth.

II Corinthians 7:14

If we confess our sins, he is faithful and just to forgive us *our* sins, and to cleanse us from all unrighteousness.

I John 1:9

Giving thanks unto the Father, which hath made us meet to be partakers of the inheritance of the saints in light:

Who hath delivered us from the power of darkness, and hath translated *us* into the kingdom of his dear Son:

In whom we have redemption through his blood, *even* the forgiveness of sins:

Colossians 1:12-14

For if ye forgive men their trespasses, your heavenly Father will also forgive you:

But if ye forgive not men their trespasses, neither will your Father forgive your trespasses.

Matthew 6:14,15

And she shall bring forth a son, and thou shalt call his name JESUS: for he shall save his people from their sins.

Matthew 1:21

Forasmuch as ye know that ye were not redeemed with corruptible things, *as* silver and gold, from your vain conversation *received* by tradition from your fathers;

But with the precious blood of Christ, as of a lamb without blemish and without spot:

I Peter 1:18,19

I acknowledged my sin unto thee, and mine iniquity have I not hid. I said, I will confess my transgressions unto the Lord; and thou forgavest the iniquity of my sin. Selah.

For this shall every one that is godly pray unto thee in a time when thou mayest be found: surely in the floods of great waters they shall not come nigh unto him.

Psalm 32:5,6

Therefore say thou unto them, Thus saith the Lord of hosts; Turn ye unto me, saith the Lord of hosts, and I will turn unto you, saith the Lord of hosts.

Zechariah 1:3

Who *is* a God like unto thee, that pardoneth iniquity, and passeth by the transgression of the remnant of his heritage? he retaineth not his anger for ever, because he delighteth *in* mercy.

He will turn again, he will have compassion upon us; he will subdue our iniquities; and thou wilt cast all their sins into the depths of the sea.

Micah 7:18,19

Therefore also now, saith the Lord, turn ye *even* to me with all your heart, and with fasting, and with weeping, and with mourning:

And rend your heart, and not your garments, and turn unto the Lord your God: for he *is* gracious and merciful, slow to anger, and of great kindness, and repenteth him of the evil.

Joel 2:12,13

And almost all things are by the law purged with blood; and without shedding of blood is no remission.

Hebrews 9:22

And be ye kind one to another, tenderhearted, forgiving one another, even as God for Christ's sake hath forgiven you.

Ephesians 4:32

Much more then, being now justified by his blood, we shall be saved from wrath through him.

For if, when we were enemies, we were reconciled to God by the death of his Son, much more, being reconciled, we shall be saved by his life.

Romans 5:9,10

He that covereth his sins shall not prosper: but whoso confesseth and forsaketh *them* shall have mercy.

Proverbs 28:13

Rescue Us From Our Enemies

He that dwelleth in the secret place of the most High shall abide under the shadow of the Almighty.

I will say of the Lord, *He is* my refuge and my fortress: my God; in him will I trust.

Surely he shall deliver thee from the snare of the fowler, *and* from the noisome pestilence.

He shall cover thee with his feathers, and under his wings shalt thou trust: his truth *shall be thy* shield and buckler.

Thou shalt not be afraid for the terror by night; *nor* for the arrow *that* flieth by day;

Nor for the pestilence *that* walketh in darkness; *nor* for the destruction *that* wasteth at noonday.

A thousand shall fall at thy side, and ten thousand at thy right hand; *but* it shall not come nigh thee.

Psalm 91:1-7

There shall no evil befall thee, neither shall any plague come nigh thy dwelling.

For he shall give his angels charge over thee, to keep thee in all thy ways.

Psalm 91:10,11

I will love thee, O Lord, my strength.

The Lord *is* my rock, and my fortress, and my deliverer; my God, my strength, in whom I will trust; my buckler, and the horn of my salvation, *and* my high tower.

I will call upon the Lord, *who is worthy* to be praised: so shall I be saved from mine enemies.

Psalm 18:1-3

For the Lord your God *is* he that goeth with you, to fight for you against your enemies, to save you.

Deuteronomy 20:4

The Lord shall cause thine enemies that rise up against thee to be smitten before thy face: they shall come out against thee one way, and flee before thee seven ways.

Deuteronomy 28:7

Though I walk in the midst of trouble, thou wilt revive me: thou shalt stretch forth thine hand against the wrath of mine enemies, and thy right hand shall save me.

Psalm 138:7

The name of the Lord *is* a strong tower: the righteous runneth into it, and is safe.

Proverbs 18:10

God *is* our refuge and strength, a very present help in trouble.

Psalm 46:1

And, behold, I *am* with thee, and will keep thee in all *places* whither thou goest, and will bring thee again into this land; for I will not leave thee, until I have done *that* which I have spoken to thee of.

Genesis 28:15

What shall we then say to these things? If God *be* for us, who *can be* against us?

Romans 8:31

But whoso hearkeneth unto me shall dwell safely, and shall be quiet from fear of evil.

Proverbs 1:33

The righteous cry, and the Lord heareth, and delivereth them out of all their troubles.

The Lord *is* nigh unto them that are of a broken heart; and saveth such as be of a contrite spirit.

Many *are* the afflictions of the righteous: but the Lord delivereth him out of them all.

Psalm 34:17-19

I will lift up mine eyes unto the hills, from whence cometh my help.

My help *cometh* from the Lord, which made heaven and earth.

Psalm 121:1,2

In the day of my trouble I will call upon thee: for thou wilt answer me.

Psalm 86:7

We are troubled on every side, yet not distressed; *we are* perplexed, but not in despair;

Persecuted, but not forsaken; cast down, but not destroyed;

II Corinthians 4:8,9

Give Us Peace In Times of Trouble

The Lord *is* my light and my salvation; whom shall I fear? the Lord *is* the strength of my life; of whom shall I be afraid?

When the wicked, *even* mine enemies and my foes, came upon me to eat up my flesh, they stumbled and fell.

Though an host should encamp against me, my heart shall not fear: though war should rise against me, in this *will* I *be* confident.

One *thing* have I desired of the Lord, that will I seek after; that I may dwell in the house of the Lord all the days of my life, to behold the beauty of the Lord, and to inquire in his temple.

For in the time of trouble he shall hide me in his pavilion: in the secret of his tabernacle shall he hide me; he shall set me up upon a rock.

Psalm 27:1-5

Wait on the Lord: be of good courage, and he shall strengthen thine heart: wait, I say, on the Lord.

Psalm 27:14

The Lord *is* my strength and my shield; my heart trusted in him, and I am helped: therefore my heart greatly rejoiceth; and with my song will I praise him.

Psalm 28:7

And the Lord, he *it is* that doth go before thee; he will be with thee, he will not fail thee, neither forsake thee: fear not, neither be dismayed.

Deuteronomy 31:8

God *is* our refuge and strength, a very present help in trouble.

Therefore will not we fear, though the earth be removed, and though the mountains be carried into the midst of the sea;

Though the waters thereof roar *and* be troubled, *though* the mountains shake with the swelling thereof. Selah.

Psalm 46:1-3

So that we may boldly say, The Lord *is* my helper, and I will not fear what man shall do unto me.

Hebrews 13:6

We are troubled on every side, yet not distressed; *we are* perplexed, but not in despair;

Persecuted, but not forsaken; cast down, but not destroyed;

II Corinthians 4:8,9

I will lift up mine eyes unto the hills, from whence cometh my help.

My help *cometh* from the Lord, which made heaven and earth.

Psalm 121:1,2

The Lord shall preserve thee from all evil: he shall preserve thy soul.

The Lord shall preserve thy going out and thy coming in from this time forth, and even for evermore.

Psalm 121:7,8

Thou wilt keep *him* in perfect peace, *whose* mind *is* stayed *on thee:* because he trusteth in thee.

Isaiah 26:3

I will say of the Lord, *He is* my refuge and my fortress: my God; in him will I trust.

Psalm 91:2

Peace I leave with you, my peace I give unto you: not as the world giveth, give I unto you. Let not your heart be troubled, neither let it be afraid.

John 14:27

Therefore I say unto you, Take no thought for your life, what ye shall eat, or what ye shall drink; nor yet for your body, what ye shall put on. Is not the life more than meat, and the body than raiment?

Behold the fowls of the air: for they sow not, neither do they reap, nor gather into barns; yet your heavenly Father feedeth them. Are ye not much better than they?

Matthew 6:25,26

Wherefore, if God so clothe the grass of the field, which today is, and tomorrow is cast into the oven, *shall he* not much more *clothe* you, O ye of little faith?

Therefore take no thought, saying, What shall we eat? or, What shall we drink? or, Wherewithal shall we be clothed?

(For after all these things do the Gentiles seek:) for your heavenly Father knoweth that ye have need of all these things.

But seek ye first the kingdom of God, and his righteousness; and all these things shall be added unto you.

Matthew 6:30-33

And fear not them which kill the body, but are not able to kill the soul: but rather fear him which is able to destroy both soul and body in hell.

Are not two sparrows sold for a far-thing? and one of them shall not fall on the ground without your Father.

But the very hairs of your head are all numbered.

Matthew 10:28-30

I will both lay me down in peace, and sleep: for thou, Lord, only makest me dwell in safety.

Psalm 4:8

And of Benjamin he said, The beloved of the Lord shall dwell in safety by him; *and the Lord* shall cover him all the day long, and he shall dwell between his shoulders.

Deuteronomy 33:12

For he shall give his angels charge over thee, to keep thee in all thy ways.

Psalm 91:11

In the multitude of my thoughts within me thy comforts delight my soul.

Psalm 94:19

But my God shall supply all your need according to his riches in glory by Christ Jesus.

Philippians 4:19

And the peace of God, which passeth all understanding, shall keep your hearts and minds through Christ Jesus.

Philippians 4:7

Not that I speak in respect of want: for I have learned, in whatsoever state I am, *therewith* to be content.

Philippians 4:11

Comfort Us When We Are Lonely

Blessed *be* God, even the Father of our Lord Jesus Christ, the Father of mercies, and the God of all comfort;

Who comforteth us in all our tribulation, that we may be able to comfort them which are in any trouble, by the comfort wherewith we ourselves are comforted of God.

II Corinthians 1:3,4

Let your conversation *be* without covetousness; *and be* content with such things as ye have: for he hath said, I will never leave thee, nor forsake thee.

Hebrews 13:5

Behold, I stand at the door, and knock: if any man hear my voice, and open the door, I will come in to him, and will sup with him, and he with me.

Revelations 3:20

Behold, I *am* the Lord, the God of all flesh: is there any thing too hard for me?

Jeremiah 32:27

And I will pray the Father, and he shall give you another Comforter, that he may abide with you for ever;

Even the Spirit of truth; whom the world cannot receive, because it seeth him not, neither knoweth him: but ye know him; for he dwelleth with you, and shall be in you.

I will not leave you comfortless: I will come to you.

John 14:16-18

He healeth the broken in heart, and bindeth up their wounds.

Psalm 147:3

For this cause I bow my knees unto the Father of our Lord Jesus Christ,

Of whom the whole family in heaven and earth is named,

That he would grant you, according to the riches of his glory, to be strengthened with might by his Spirit in the inner man;

Ephesians 3:14-16

Whom have I in heaven *but thee*? and *there is* none upon earth *that* I desire beside thee.

My flesh and my heart faileth: *but* God *is* the strength of my heart, and my portion for ever.

Psalm 73:25,26

Thou wilt keep *him* in perfect peace, *whose* mind *is* stayed *on thee*: because he trusteth in thee.

Isaiah 26:3

Nevertheless I tell you the truth; It is expedient for you that I go away: for if I go not away, the Comforter will not come unto you; but if I depart, I will send him unto you.

John 16:7

For with God nothing shall be impossible.

Luke 1:37

Comfort Us When We Grieve

For I am persuaded, that neither death, nor life, nor angels, nor principalities, nor powers, nor things present, nor things to come,

Nor height, nor depth, nor any other creature, shall be able to separate us from the love of God, which is in Christ Jesus our Lord.

Romans 8:38,39

Sing, O heavens; and be joyful, O earth; and break forth into singing, O mountains: for the Lord hath comforted his people, and will have mercy upon his afflicted.

Isaiah 49:13

Blessed *are* they that mourn: for they shall be comforted.

Matthew 5:4

And the ransomed of the Lord shall return, and come to Zion with songs and everlasting joy upon their heads: they shall obtain joy and gladness, and sorrow and sighing shall flee away.

Isaiah 35:10

He healeth the broken in heart, and bindeth up their wounds.

Psalm 147:3

They that sow in tears shall reap in joy.

Psalm 126:5

I love the Lord, because he hath heard my voice *and* my supplications.

Because he hath inclined his ear unto me, therefore will I call upon *him* as long as I live.

The sorrows of death compassed me, and the pains of hell gat hold upon me: I found trouble and sorrow.

Then called I upon the name of the Lord; O Lord, I beseech thee, deliver my soul.

Psalm 116:1-4

I cried unto God with my voice, *even* unto God with my voice; and he gave ear unto me.

Psalm 77:1

Thou, which hast shewed me great and sore troubles, shalt quicken me again, and shalt bring me up again from the depths of the earth.

Thou shalt increase my greatness, and comfort me on every side.

Psalm 71:20,21

I will not leave you comfortless: I will come to you.

John 14:18

For all things *are* for your sakes, that the abundant grace might through the thanksgiving of many redound to the glory of God.

For which cause we faint not; but though our outward man perish, yet the inward *man* is renewed day by day.

For our light affliction, which is but for a moment, worketh for us a far more exceeding *and* eternal weight of glory;

While we look not at the things which are seen, but at the things which are not seen: for the things which are seen *are* temporal; but the things which are not seen *are* eternal.

II Corinthians 4:15-18

Yea, though I walk through the valley of the shadow of death, I will fear no evil: for thou *art* with me; thy rod and thy staff they comfort me.

Psalm 23:4

Protect Us

But even the very hairs of your head are all numbered. Fear not therefore: ye are of more value than many sparrows.
Luke 12:7

Consider the ravens: for they neither sow nor reap; which neither have storehouse nor barn; and God feedeth them: how much more are ye better than the fowls?
Luke 12:24

If then God so clothe the grass, which is today in the field, and tomorrow is cast into the oven; how much more *will he clothe* you, O ye of little faith?
Luke 12:28

Since thou wast precious in my sight, thou hast been honourable, and I have loved thee: therefore will I give men for thee, and people for thy life.
Fear not: for I *am* with thee: I will bring thy seed from the east, and gather thee from the west;
Isaiah 43:4,5

Keep me as the apple of the eye, hide me under the shadow of thy wings,
Psalm 17:8

They prevented me in the day of my calamity: but the Lord was my stay.

He brought me forth also into a large place; he delivered me, because he delighted in me.

Psalm 18:18,19

For the Lord taketh pleasure in his people: he will beautify the meek with salvation.

Psalm 149:4

But the Lord is faithful, who shall stablish you, and keep *you* from evil.

II Thessalonians 3:3

One *thing* have I desired of the Lord, that will I seek after; that I may dwell in the house of the Lord all the days of my life, to behold the beauty of the Lord, and to inquire in his temple.

For in the time of trouble he shall hide me in his pavilion: in the secret of his tabernacle shall he hide me; he shall set me up upon a rock.

And now shall mine head be lifted up above mine enemies round about me: therefore will I offer in his tabernacle sacrifices of joy; I will sing, yea, I will sing praises unto the Lord.

Psalm 27:4-6

Wait on the Lord: be of good courage, and he shall strengthen thine heart: wait, I say, on the Lord.

Psalm 27:14

Deliver me, O Lord, from the evil man: preserve me from the violent man;

Which imagine mischiefs in *their* heart; continually are they gathered together *for* war.

They have sharpened their tongues like a serpent; adders' poison *is* under their lips. Selah.

Keep me, O Lord, from the hands of the wicked; preserve me from the violent man; who have purposed to overthrow my goings.

Psalm 140:1-4

The Lord shall preserve thee from all evil: he shall preserve thy soul.

The Lord shall preserve thy going out and thy coming in from this time forth, and even for evermore.

Psalm 121:7,8

The Lord *is* on my side; I will not fear: what can man do unto me?

Psalm 118:6

Heal Us When We're Sick

Heal me, O Lord, and I shall be healed; save me, and I shall be saved: for thou *art* my praise.

Jeremiah 17:14

Bless the Lord, O my soul, and forget not all his benefits:

Who forgiveth all thine iniquities; who healeth all thy diseases;

Psalm 103:2,3

And said, If thou wilt diligently hearken to the voice of the Lord thy God, and wilt do that which is right in his sight, and wilt give ear to his commandments, and keep all his statutes, I will put none of these diseases upon thee, which I have brought upon the Egyptians: for I *am* the Lord that healeth thee.

Exodus 15:26

And the prayer of faith shall save the sick, and the Lord shall raise him up; and if he have committed sins, they shall be forgiven him.

James 5:15

O Lord my God, I cried unto thee, and thou hast healed me.

Psalm 30:2

And Jesus went forth, and saw a great multitude, and was moved with compassion toward them, and he healed their sick.

Matthew 14:14

And, behold, there came a leper and worshipped him, saying, Lord, if thou wilt, thou canst make me clean.

And Jesus put forth *his* hand, and touched him, saying, I will; be thou clean. And immediately his leprosy was cleansed.

Matthew 8:2,3

But Jesus turned him about, and when he saw her, he said, Daughter, be of good comfort; thy faith hath made thee whole. And the woman was made whole from that hour.

Matthew 9:22

The Lord will strengthen him upon the bed of languishing: thou wilt make all his bed in his sickness.

Psalm 41:3

And ye shall serve the Lord your God, and He shall bless thy bread, and thy water; and I will take sickness away from the midst of thee.

Exodus 23:25

Behold, I will bring it health and cure, and I will cure them and will reveal unto them the abundance of peace and truth.

Jeremiah 33:6

For I will restore health unto thee, and I will heal thee of thy wounds, saith the Lord; because they called thee an Outcast, *saying*, This *is* Zion, whom no man seeketh after.

Jeremiah 30:17

Then shall thy light break forth as the morning, and thine health shall spring forth speedily: and thy righteousness shall go before thee; the glory of the Lord shall be thy rereward.

Isaiah 58:8

And these signs shall follow them that believe; In my name shall they cast out devils; they shall speak with new tongues;
They shall take up serpents; and if they drink any deadly thing, it shall not hurt them; they shall lay hands on the sick, and they shall recover.

Mark 16:17,18

Why art thou cast down, O my soul? and why art thou disquieted within me? hope thou in God: for I shall yet praise him, *who is* the health of my countenance, and my God.

Psalm 42:11

Strengthen Us When We Are Discouraged

The Lord *is* my strength and my shield; my heart trusted in him, and I am helped: therefore my heart greatly rejoiceth; and with my song will I praise him.

Psalm 28:7

The Lord *is* my light and my salvation; whom shall I fear? the Lord *is* the strength of my life; of whom shall I be afraid?

Psalm 27:1

And the Lord, he *it is* that doth go before thee; he will be with thee, he will not fail thee, neither forsake thee: fear not, neither be dismayed.

Deuteronomy 31:8

Why art thou cast down, O my soul? and why art thou disquieted within me? hope thou in God: for I shall yet praise him, *who is* the health of my countenance, and my God.

Psalm 42:11

But the salvation of the righteous *is* of the Lord: *he is* their strength in the time of trouble.

Psalm 37:39

My flesh and my heart faileth: *but* God *is* the strength of my heart, and my portion for ever.

Psalm 73:26

I can do all things through Christ which strengtheneth me.

Phillippians 4:13

Peace I leave with you, my peace I give unto you: not as the world giveth, give I unto you. Let not your heart be troubled, neither let it be afraid.

John 14:27

But thou, O Lord, *art* a shield for me; my glory, and the lifter up of mine head.

I cried unto the Lord with my voice, and he heard me out of his holy hill. Selah.

I laid me down and slept; I awaked; for the Lord sustained me.

I will not be afraid of ten thousands of people, that have set *themselves* against me round about.

Psalm 3:3-6

Thou *art* my hiding place; thou shalt preserve me from trouble; thou shalt compass me about with songs of deliverance. Selah.

Psalm 32:7

This people have I formed for myself; they shall shew forth my praise.

Isaiah 43:21

For whatsoever is born of God overcometh the world: and this is the victory that overcometh the world, *even* our faith.

I John 5:4

The eternal God *is thy* refuge, and underneath *are* the everlasting arms: and he shall thrust out the enemy from before thee; and shall say, Destroy *them*.

Deuteronomy 33:27

For thou hast been a strength to the poor, a strength to the needy in his distress, a refuge from the storm, a shadow from the heat, when the blast of the terrible ones *is* as a storm *against* the wall.

Isaiah 25:4

Answer Our Prayers

For verily I say unto you, That whosoever shall say unto this mountain, Be thou removed, and be thou cast into the sea; and shall not doubt in his heart, but shall believe that those things which he saith shall come to pass; he shall have whatsoever he saith.

Therefore I say unto you, What things soever ye desire, when ye pray, believe that ye receive *them,* and ye shall have *them.*

Mark 11:23,24

And this is the confidence that we have in him, that, if we ask any thing according to his will, he heareth us:

And if we know that he hear us, whatsoever we ask, we know that we have the petitions that we desired of him.

I John 5:14,15

If my people, which are called by my name, shall humble themselves, and pray, and seek my face, and turn from their wicked ways; then will I hear from heaven, and will forgive their sin, and will heal their land.

II Chronicles 7:14

And whatsoever we ask, we receive of him, because we keep his commandments, and do those things that are pleasing in his sight.

I John 3:22

Therefore I will look unto the Lord; I will wait for the God of my salvation: my God will hear me.

Micah 7:7

Again I say unto you, That if two of you shall agree on earth as touching any thing that they shall ask, it shall be done for them of my Father which is in heaven.

Matthew 18:19

The Lord *is* far from the wicked: but he heareth the prayer of the righteous.

Proverbs 15:29

And I say unto you, Ask, and it shall be given you; seek, and ye shall find; knock, and it shall be opened unto you.

For every one that asketh receiveth; and he that seeketh findeth; and to him that knocketh it shall be opened.

If a son shall ask bread of any of you that is a father, will he give him a stone? or if *he ask* a fish, will he for a fish give him a serpent?

Or if he shall ask an egg, will he offer him a scorpion?

If ye then, being evil, know how to give good gifts unto your children: how much more shall *your* heavenly Father give the Holy Spirit to them that ask him?

Luke 11:9-13

Then shall ye call upon me, and ye shall go and pray unto me, and I will hearken unto you.

Jeremiah 29:12

Confess *your* faults one to another, and pray one for another, that ye may be healed. The effectual fervent prayer of a righteous man availeth much.

James 5:16

Thou hast given him his heart's desire, and hast not withholden the request of his lips. Selah.

Psalms 21:2

Call unto me, and I will answer thee, and shew thee great and mighty things, which thou knowest not.

Jeremiah 33:3

And it shall come to pass, that before they call, I will answer; and while they are yet speaking, I will hear.

Isaiah 65:24

Evening, and morning, and at noon, will I pray, and cry aloud: and he shall hear my voice.

Psalm 55:17

And whatsoever ye shall ask in my name, that will I do, that the Father may be glorified in the Son.

If ye shall ask any thing in my name, I will do *it*.

John 14:13,14

The righteous cry, and the Lord heareth, and delivereth them out of all their troubles.

Psalm 34:17

He shall call upon me, and I will answer him: I *will be* with him in trouble; I will deliver him, and honour him.

Psalm 91:15

Bless Us With His Presence

Thou hast beset me behind and before, and laid thine hand upon me.

Such knowledge *is* too wonderful for me; it is high, I cannot *attain* unto it.

Whither shall I go from thy spirit? or whither shall I flee from thy presence?

If I ascend up into heaven, thou *art* there: if I make my bed in hell, behold, thou *art there*.

If I take the wings of the morning, *and* dwell in the uttermost parts of the sea;

Even there shall thy hand lead me, and thy right hand shall hold me.

Psalm 139:5-10

Be strong and of a good courage, fear not, nor be afraid of them: for the Lord thy God, he *it is* that doth go with thee; he will not *fail* thee, nor forsake thee.

Deuteronomy 31:6

And he said, My presence shall go *with thee*, and I will give thee rest.

Exodus 33:14

Then shalt thou call, and the Lord shall answer; thou shalt cry, and he shall say, Here I *am*. If thou take away from the midst of thee the yoke, the putting forth of the finger, and speaking vanity;

Isaiah 58:9

Surely the righteous shall give thanks unto thy name: the upright shall dwell in thy presence.

Psalm 140:13

And he went out to meet Asa, and said unto him, Hear ye me, Asa, and all Judah and Benjamin; the Lord *is* with you, while ye be with Him; and if ye seek Him, He will be found of you; but if ye forsake Him, He will forsake you.

II Chronicles 15:2

O come, let us sing unto the Lord: let us make a joyful noise to the rock of our salvation.
Let us come before his presence with thanksgiving, and make a joyful noise unto him with psalms.

Psalm 95:1,2

Cast me not away from thy presence; and take not thy holy spirit from me.

Psalm 51:11

Now unto him that is able to keep you from falling, and to present *you* faultless before the presence of his glory with exceeding joy,

To the only wise God our Saviour, *be* glory and majesty, dominion and power, both now and ever. Amen.

Jude 24,25

That which we have seen and heard declare we unto you, that ye also may have fellowship with us: and truly our fellowship *is* with the Father, and with his Son Jesus Christ.

I John 1:3

Finally, brethren, farewell. Be perfect, be of good comfort, be of one mind, live in peace; and the God of love and peace shall be with you.

II Corinthians 13:11

For in him we live, and move, and have our being; as certain also of your own poets have said, For we are also his offspring.

Acts 17:28

Fear thou not; for I *am* with thee: be not dismayed; for I *am* thy God: I will strengthen thee; yea, I will help thee; yea, I will uphold thee with the right hand of my righteousness.

Isaiah 41:10

Thou wilt shew me the path of life: in thy presence *is* fulness of joy; at thy right hand *there are* pleasures for evermore.

Psalm 16:11

Guide Us Day-By-Day

Howbeit when he, the Spirit of truth, is come, he will guide you into all truth: for he shall not speak of himself; but whatsoever he shall hear, *that* shall he speak: and he will shew you things to come.

John 16:13

And thine ears shall hear a word behind thee, saying This *is* the way, walk ye in it, when ye turn to the right hand, and when ye turn to the left.

Isaiah 30:21

I will instruct thee and teach thee in the way which thou shalt go: I will guide thee with mine eye.

Psalm 32:8

Have not I commanded thee? Be strong and of a good courage; be not afraid, neither be thou dismayed: for the Lord thy God *is* with thee whithersoever thou goest.

Joshua 1:9

Yea, though I walk through the valley of the shadow of death, I will fear no evil: for thou *art* with me; thy rod and thy staff they comfort me.

Psalm 23:4

For this God *is* our God for ever and ever: he will be our guide *even* unto death.

Psalm 48:14

The steps of a *good* man are ordered by the Lord: and he delighteth in his way.

Psalm 37:23

He found him in a desert land, and in the waste howling wilderness; he led him about, he instructed him, he kept him as the apple of his eye.

As an eagle stirreth up her nest, fluttereth over her young, spreadeth abroad her wings, taketh them, beareth them on her wings:

So the Lord alone did lead him, and *there was* no strange god with him.

Deuteronomy 32:10-12

And I will put my spirit within you, and cause you to walk in my statutes, and ye shall keep my judgments, and do *them*.

Ezekiel 36:27

Then shalt thou call, and the Lord shall answer; thou shalt cry, and he shall say, Here I *am*. If thou take away from the midst of thee the yoke, the putting forth of the finger, and speaking vanity;

And *if* thou draw out thy soul to the hungry, and satisfy the afflicted soul; then shall thy light rise in obscurity, and thy darkness *be* as the noonday:

And the Lord shall guide thee continually, and satisfy thy soul in drought, and make fat thy bones: and thou shalt be like a watered garden, and like a spring of water, whose waters fail not.

Isaiah 58:9-11

They shall not hunger nor thirst; neither shall the heat nor sun smite them: for he that hath mercy on them shall lead them, even by the springs of water shall he guide them.

Isaiah 49:10

And I will bring the blind by a way *that* they knew not: I will lead them in paths *that* they have not known: I will make darkness light before them, and crooked things straight. These things will I do unto them, and not forsake them.

Isaiah 42:16

A man's heart deviseth his way: but the Lord directeth his steps.

Proverbs 16:9

In all thy ways acknowledge him, and he shall direct thy paths.

Proverbs 3:6

Thou shalt guide me with thy counsel, and afterward receive me *to* glory.

Psalm 73:24

Being confident of this very thing, that he which hath begun a good work in you will perform *it* until the day of Jesus Christ.

Philippians 1:6

For as many as are led by the Spirit of God, they are the sons of God.

Romans 8:14

Teach Us His Will

Trust in the Lord with all thine heart; and lean not unto thine own understanding.

In all thy ways acknowledge him, and he shall direct thy paths.

Proverbs 3:5,6

I beseech you therefore, brethren, by the mercies of God, that ye present your bodies a living sacrifice, holy, acceptable unto God, *which is* your reasonable service.

And be not conformed to this world: but be ye transformed by the renewing of your mind, that ye may prove what *is* that good, and acceptable, and perfect, will of God.

Romans 12:1,2

Likewise the Spirit also helpeth our infirmities: for we know not what we should pray for as we ought: but the Spirit itself maketh intercession for us with groanings which cannot be uttered.

And he that searcheth the hearts knoweth what *is* the mind of the Spirit, because he maketh intercession for the saints according to *the will of* God.

Romans 8:26,27

Then spake Jesus again unto them, saying, I am the light of the world: he that followeth me shall not walk in darkness, but shall have the light of life.

John 8:12

I have set the Lord always before me: because *he is* at my right hand, I shall not be moved.

Psalm 16:8

And I will put my spirit within you, and cause you to walk in my statutes, and ye shall keep my judgments, and do *them*.

Ezekiel 36:27

And many people shall go and say, Come ye, and let us go up to the mountain of the Lord, to the house of the God of Jacob; and he will teach us of his ways, and we will walk in his paths: for out of Zion shall go forth the law, and the word of the Lord from Jerusalem.

Isaiah 2:3

For the commandment *is* a lamp; and the law *is* light; and reproofs of instruction are the way of life:

Proverbs 6:23

For this cause we also, since the day we heard *it*, do not cease to pray for you, and to desire that ye might be filled with the knowledge of his will in all wisdom and spiritual understanding;

Colossians 1:9

Grant Us Wisdom

My son, if thou wilt receive my words, and hide my commandments with thee;

So that thou incline thine ear unto wisdom, *and* apply thine heart to understanding;

Yea, if thou criest after knowledge, *and* liftest up thy voice for understanding;

If thou seekest her as silver, and searchest for her as *for* hid treasures;

Then shalt thou understand the fear of the Lord, and find the knowledge of God.

For the Lord giveth wisdom: out of his mouth *cometh* knowledge and understanding.

He layeth up sound wisdom for the righteous: *he is* a buckler to them that walk uprightly.

Proverbs 2:1-7

If any of you lack wisdom, let him ask of God, that giveth to all *men* liberally, and upbraideth not; and it shall be given him.

James 1:5

For *God* giveth to a man that *is* good in his sight wisdom, and knowledge, and joy: but to the sinner he giveth travail, to gather and to heap up, that he may give to *him that is* good before God. This also *is* vanity and vexation of spirit.

Ecclesiastes 2:26

Only the Lord give thee wisdom and understanding, and give thee charge concerning Israel, that thou mayest keep the law of the Lord thy God.

I Chronicles 22:12

That the God of our Lord Jesus Christ, the Father of glory, may give unto you the spirit of wisdom and revelation in the knowledge of him:

Ephesians 1:17

So teach *us* to number our days, that we may apply *our* hearts unto wisdom.

Psalm 90:12

He that getteth wisdom loveth his own soul: he that keepeth understanding shall find good.

Proverbs 19:8

And that from a child thou hast known the holy scriptures, which are able to make thee wise unto salvation through faith which is in Christ Jesus.

II Timothy 3:15

Reprove not a scorner, lest he hate thee: rebuke a wise man, and he will love thee.

Give *instruction* to a wise *man*, and he will be yet wiser: teach a just *man*, and he will increase in learning.

The fear of the Lord *is* the beginning of wisdom: and the knowledge of the holy *is* understanding.

Proverbs 9:8-10

A man's heart deviseth his way: but the Lord directeth his steps.

Proverbs 16:9

Counsel *is* mine, and sound wisdom: I *am* understanding; I have strength.

Proverbs 8:14

But *there is* a spirit in man: and the inspiration of the Almighty giveth them understanding.

Job 32:8

GOD CARES ENOUGH TO ...
Teach Us Obedience

But this thing commanded I them, saying, Obey my voice, and I will be your God, and ye shall be my people: and walk ye in all the ways that I have commanded you, that it may be well unto you.

Jeremiah 7:23

Thou shalt keep therefore his statutes, and his commandments, which I command thee this day, that it may go well with thee, and with thy children after thee, and that thou mayest prolong *thy* days upon the earth, which the Lord thy God giveth thee, for ever.

Deuteronomy 4:40

Now therefore, if ye will obey my voice indeed, and keep my covenant, then ye shall be a peculiar treasure unto me above all people: for all the earth *is* mine.

Exodus 19:5

Beloved, if our heart condemn us not, *then* have we confidence toward God.

And whatsoever we ask, we receive of him, because we keep his commandments, and do those things that are pleasing in his sight.

I John 3:21,22

Now no chastening for the present seemeth to be joyous, but grievous: nevertheless afterward it yieldeth the peaceable fruit of righteousness unto them which are exercised thereby.

Hebrews 12:11

And keep the charge of the Lord thy God, to walk in his ways, to keep his statutes, and his commandments, and his judgments, and his testimonies, as it is written in the law of Moses, that thou mayest prosper in all that thou doest, and whithersoever thou turnest thyself:

I Kings 2:3

O Lord, rebuke me not in thy wrath: neither chasten me in thy hot displeasure.

For thine arrows stick fast in me, and thy hand presseth me sore.

There is no soundness in my flesh because of thine anger; neither *is there any* rest in my bones because of my sin.

For mine iniquities are gone over mine head: as an heavy burden they are too heavy for me.

Psalm 38:1-4

For I will declare mine iniquity; I will be sorry for my sin.

Psalm 38:18

Forsake me not, O Lord: O my God, be not far from me.

Make haste to help me, O Lord my salvation.

Psalm 38:21,22

Though he fall, he shall not be utterly cast down: for the Lord upholdeth *him with* his hand.

Psalm 37:24

And if thou wilt walk in my ways, to keep my statutes and my commandments, as thy father David did walk, then I will lengthen thy days.

I Kings 3:14

And Samuel said, Hath the Lord *as great* delight in burnt offerings and sacrifices, as in obeying the voice of the Lord? Behold, to obey *is* better than sacrifice, *and* to hearken than the fat of rams.

I Samuel 15:22

Behold, I set before you this day a blessing and a curse;

A blessing, if ye obey the commandments of the Lord your God, which I command you this day:

And a curse, if ye will not obey the commandments of the Lord your God, but turn aside out of the way which I command you this day, to go after other Gods, which ye have not known.

Deuteronomy 11:26-28

But your iniquities have separated between you and your God, and your sins have hid *his* face from you, that he will not hear.

Isaiah 59:2

If ye be willing and obedient, ye shall eat the good of the land:

Isaiah 1:19

Evil men understand not judgment: but they that seek the Lord understand all *things*.

Proverbs 28:5

As many as I love, I rebuke and chasten: be zealous therefore, and repent.

Revelation 3:19

Show Us Mercy and Grace

Let us therefore come boldly unto the throne of grace, that we may obtain mercy, and find grace to help in time of need.

Hebrews 4:16

Let the wicked forsake his way, and the unrighteous man his thoughts: and let him return unto the Lord, and he will have mercy upon him; and to our God, for he will abundantly pardon.

Isaiah 55:7

And of his fulness have all we received, and grace for grace.

For the law was given by Moses, *but* grace and truth came by Jesus Christ.

John 1:16,17

O give thanks unto the Lord; for *he is* good: because his mercy *endureth* for ever.

Psalm 118:1

For the Lord *is* good; his mercy *is* everlasting; and his truth *endureth* to all generations.

Psalm 100:5

For the Lord God *is* a sun and shield: the Lord will give grace and glory: no good *thing* will he withhold from them that walk uprightly.

Psalm 84:11

Many sorrows *shall be* to the wicked: but he that trusteth in the Lord, mercy shall compass him about.

Psalm 32:10

Behold, the eye of the Lord *is* upon them that fear him, upon them that hope in his mercy;

Psalm 33:18

But I have trusted in thy mercy; my heart shall rejoice in thy salvation.

I will sing unto the Lord, because he hath dealt bountifully with me.

Psalm 13:5,6

And the Lord thy God will bring thee into the land which thy fathers possessed, and thou shalt possess it; and he will do thee good, and multiply thee above thy fathers.

Deuteronomy 30:5

Blessed *is* the man that trusteth in the Lord, and whose hope the Lord is.

Jeremiah 17:7

He hath not dealt with us after our sins; nor rewarded us according to our iniquities.

For as the heaven is high above the earth, *so* great is his mercy toward them that fear him.

Psalm 103:10,11

For he saith to Moses, I will have mercy on whom I will have mercy, and I will have compassion on whom I will have compassion.

So then *it is* not of him that willeth, nor of him that runneth, but of God that sheweth mercy.

Romans 9:15,16

When I said, My foot slippeth; thy mercy, O Lord, held me up.

Psalm 94:18

O Lord, rebuke me not in thine anger, neither chasten me in thy hot displeasure.

Have mercy upon me, O Lord; for I *am* weak: O Lord, heal me; for my bones are vexed.

My soul is also sore vexed: but thou, O Lord, how long?

Psalm 6:1-3

Give Us Love For Others

As the Father hath loved me, so have I loved you: continue ye in my love.

If ye keep my commandments, ye shall abide in my love; even as I have kept my Father's commandments, and abide in his love.

These things have I spoken unto you, that my joy might remain in you, and *that* your joy might be full.

This is my commandment, That ye love one another, as I have loved you.

John 15:9-12

A new commandment I give unto you, That ye love one another; as I have loved you, that ye also love one another.

By this shall all *men* know that ye are my disciples, if ye have love one to another.

John 13:34,35

Ye call me Master and Lord: and ye say well; for *so* I am.

If I then, *your* Lord and Master, have washed your feet; ye also ought to wash one another's feet.

For I have given you an example, that ye should do as I have done to you.

Verily, verily, I say unto you, The servant is not greater than his lord; neither he that is sent greater than he that sent him.

If ye know these things, happy are ye if ye do them.

John 13:13-17

And the Lord make you to increase and abound in love one toward another, and toward all *men,* even as we *do* toward you:

I Thessalonians 3:12

Ye have heard that it hath been said, Thou shalt love thy neighbor, and hate thine enemy.

But I say unto you, Love your enemies, bless them that curse you, do good to them that hate you, and pray for them which despitefully use you, and persecute you;

That ye may be the children of your Father which is in heaven: for he maketh his sun to rise on the evil and on the good, and sendeth rain on the just and on the unjust.

For if ye love them which love you, what reward have ye? do not even the publicans the same?

And if ye salute your brethren only, what do ye more *than others*? do not even the publicans so?

Be ye therefore perfect, even as your Father which is in heaven is perfect.

Matthew 5:43-48

Beloved, let us love one another: for love is of God; and every one that loveth is born of God, and knoweth God.

I John 4:7

Finally, *be ye* all of one mind, having compassion one of another, love as brethren, *be* pitiful, *be* courteous:

I Peter 3:8

And above all things have fervent charity among yourselves: for charity shall cover the multitude of sins.

I Peter 4:8

A friend loveth at all times, and a brother is born for adversity.

Proverbs 17:17

We know that we have passed from death unto life, because we love the brethren. He that loveth not *his* brother abideth in death.

I John 3:14

Beloved, if God so loved us, we ought also to love one another.

No man hath seen God at any time. If we love one another, God dwelleth in us, and his love is perfected in us.

I John 4:11,12

God *is* faithful, by whom ye were called unto the fellowship of his Son Jesus Christ our Lord.

Now I beseech you, brethren, by the name of our Lord Jesus Christ, that ye all speak the same thing, and *that* there be no divisions among you; but *that* ye be perfectly joined together in the same mind and in the same judgment.

I Corinthians 1:9,10

Behold, how good and how pleasant *it is* for brethren to dwell together in unity!

It is like the precious ointment upon the head, that ran down upon the beard, *even* Aaron's beard: that went down to the skirts of his garments;

As the dew of Hermon, *and as the dew* that descended upon the mountains of Zion: for there the Lord commanded the blessing, *even* life for evermore.

Psalm 133:1-3

Reward Us When We Are Humble

Likewise, ye younger, submit yourselves unto the elder. Yea, all *of you* be subject one to another, and be clothed with humility: for God resisteth the proud, and giveth grace to the humble.

Humble yourselves therefore under the mighty hand of God, that he may exalt you in due time.

I Peter 5:5,6

Two men went up into the temple to pray; the one a Pharisee, and the other a publican.

The Pharisee stood and prayed thus with himself, God, I thank thee, that I am not as other men *are,* extortioners, unjust, adulterers, or even as this publican.

I fast twice in the week, I give tithes of all that I possess.

And the publican, standing afar off, would not lift up so much as *his* eyes unto heaven, but smote upon his breast, saying, God be merciful to me a sinner.

I tell you, this man went down to his house justified *rather* than the other: for every one that exalteth himself shall be abased; and he that humbleth himself shall be exalted.

Luke 18:10-14

Whosoever therefore shall humble himself as this little child, the same is greatest in the kingdom of heaven.

Matthew 18:4

But he giveth more grace. Wherefore he saith, God resisteth the proud, but giveth grace unto the humble.

James 4:6

Humble yourselves in the sight of the Lord, and he shall lift you up.

James 4:10

A man's pride shall bring him low: but honour shall uphold the humble in spirit.

Proverbs 29:23

The meek will he guide in judgment: and the meek will he teach his way.

Psalms 25:9

Blessed *are* the poor in spirit: for theirs is the kingdom of heaven.

Matthew 5:3

Blessed *are* the meek: for they shall inherit the earth.

Matthew 5:5

For all those *things* hath mine hand made, and all those *things* have been, saith the Lord: but to this *man* will I look, *even* to *him that is* poor and of a contrite spirit, and trembleth at my word.

Isaiah 66:2

Better *is* the end of a thing than the beginning thereof: *and* the patient in spirit *is* better than the proud in spirit.

Ecclesiastes 7:8

By humility *and* the fear of the Lord *are* riches, and honour, and life.

Proverbs 22:4

Though the Lord *be* high, yet hath he respect unto the lowly: but the proud he knoweth afar off.

Psalm 138:6

For whosoever exalteth himself shall be abased; and he that humbleth himself shall be exalted.

Luke 14:11

Furthermore we have had fathers of our flesh which corrected *us*, and we gave *them* reverence: shall we not much rather be in subjection unto the Father of spirits, and live?

Hebrews 12:9

For I say, through the grace given unto me, to every man that is among you, not to think *of himself* more highly than he ought to think; but to think soberly, according as God hath dealt to every man the measure of faith.

Romans 12:3

Adorn Us As His Bride

I will greatly rejoice in the Lord, my soul shall be joyful in my God; for he hath clothed me with the garments of salvation, he hath covered me with the robe of righteousness, as a bridegroom decketh *himself* with ornaments, and as a bride adorneth *herself* with her jewels.

For as the earth bringeth forth her bud, and as the garden causeth the things that are sown in it to spring forth; so the Lord God will cause righteousness and praise to spring forth before all the nations.

Isaiah 61:10,11

For *as* a young man marrieth a virgin, *so* shall thy sons marry thee: and *as* the bridegroom rejoiceth over the bride, *so* shall thy God rejoice over thee.

Isaiah 62:5

Lift up thine eyes round about, and behold: all these gather themselves together, *and* come to thee. *As* I live, saith the Lord, thou shalt surely clothe thee with them all, as with an ornament, and bind them *on thee*, as a bride *doeth*.

Isaiah 49:18

For thy Maker *is* thine husband; the Lord of hosts *is* his name; and thy Redeemer the Holy One of Israel; The God of the whole earth shall he be called.

Isaiah 54:5

And the Spirit and the bride say, Come. And let him that heareth say, Come. And let him that is athirst come. And whosoever will, let him take the water of life freely.

Revelation 22:17

Let us be glad and rejoice, and give honour to him: for the marriage of the Lamb is come, and his wife hath made herself ready.

And to her was granted that she should be arrayed in fine linen, clean and white: for the fine linen is the righteousness of saints.

Revelation 19:7,8

He that hath the bride is the bridegroom: but the friend of the bridegroom, which standeth and heareth him, rejoiceth greatly because of the bridegroom's voice: this my joy therefore is fulfilled.

John 3:29

AND I saw a new heaven and a new earth: for the first heaven and the first earth were passed away; and there was no more sea.

And I John saw the holy city, new Jerusalem, coming down from God out of heaven, prepared as a bride adorned for her husband.

Revelation 21:1-2

There is no speech nor language, *where* their voice is not heard.

Their line is gone out through all the earth, and their words to the end of the world. In them hath he set a tabernacle for the sun,

Which *is* as a bridegroom coming out of his chamber, *and* rejoiceth as a strong man to run a race.

Psalm 19:3-5

Behold, the Lord hath proclaimed unto the end of the world, Say ye to the daughter of Zion, Behold, thy salvation cometh; behold, his reward *is* with him, and his work before him.

And they shall call them, The holy people, The redeemed of the Lord: and thou shalt be called, Sought out, A city not forsaken.

Isaiah 62:11,12

The glory of this latter house shall be greater than of the former, saith the Lord of hosts: and in this place will I give peace, saith the Lord of hosts.

Haggai 2:9

Share His Lordship With Us

What is man, that thou art mindful of him? and the son of man, that thou visitest him?

For thou hast made him a little lower than the angels, and hast crowned him with glory and honour.

Thou madest him to have dominion over the works of thy hands; thou hast put all *things* under his feet:

All sheep and oxen, yea, and the beasts of the field;

The fowl of the air, and the fish of the sea, *and whatsoever* passeth through the paths of the seas.

O Lord our Lord, how excellent *is* thy name in all the earth!

Psalms 8:4-9

And I appoint unto you a kingdom, as my Father hath appointed unto me;

That ye may eat and drink at my table in my kingdom, and sit on thrones judging the twelve tribes of Israel.

Luke 22:29,30

To him that overcometh will I grant to sit with me in my throne, even as I also overcame, and am set down with my Father in his throne.

Revelation 3:21

But ye *are* a chosen generation, a royal priesthood, an holy nation, a peculiar people; that ye should shew forth the praises of him who hath called you out of darkness into his marvellous light;

I Peter 2:9

Blessed and holy *is* he that hath part in the first resurrection: on such the second death hath no power, but they shall be priests of God and of Christ, and shall reign with him a thousand years.

Revelation 20:6

His lord said unto him, Well done, *thou* good and faithful servant: thou hast been faithful over a few things, I will make thee ruler over many things: enter thou into the joy of thy lord.

Matthew 25:21

Now therefore, if ye will obey my voice indeed, and keep my covenant, then ye shall be a peculiar treasure unto me above all people: for all the earth *is* mine:

And ye shall be unto me a kingdom of priests, and an holy nation. These *are* the words which thou shalt speak unto the children of Israel.

Exodus 19:5,6

And from Jesus Christ, *who is* the faithful witness, *and* the first begotten of the dead, and the prince of the kings of the earth. Unto him that loved us, and washed us from our sins in his own blood,

And hath made us kings and priests unto God and his Father; to him *be* glory and dominion for ever and ever. Amen.

Revelation 1:5,6

But this *man*, because he continueth ever, hath an unchangeable priesthood.

Wherefore he is able also to save them to the uttermost that come unto God by him, seeing he ever liveth to make intercession for them.

Hebrews 7:24,25

Now therefore ye are no more strangers and foreigners, but fellowcitizens with the saints, and of the household of God;

Ephesians 2:19

And God blessed Noah and his sons, and said unto them, Be fruitful, and multiply, and replenish the earth.

And the fear of you and the dread of you shall be upon every beast of the earth, and upon every fowl of the air, upon all that moveth *upon* the earth, and upon all the fishes of the sea; into your hand are they delivered.

Genesis 9:1,2

And I saw thrones, and they sat upon them, and judgment was given unto them: and *I saw* the souls of them that were beheaded for the witness of Jesus, and for the word of God, and which had not worshipped the beast, neither his image, neither had received *his* mark upon their foreheads, or in their hands; and they lived and reigned with Christ a thousand years.

Revelation 20:4

Make Us His Holy Temple

I am crucified with Christ: nevertheless I live; yet not I, but Christ liveth in me: and the life which I now live in the flesh I live by the faith of the Son of God, who loved me, and gave himself for me.

Galatians 2:20

And what agreement hath the temple of God with idols? for ye are the temple of the living God; as God hath said, I will dwell in them, and walk in *them*; and I will be their God, and they shall be my people.

II Corinthians 6:16

Know ye not that ye are the temple of God, and *that* the Spirit of God dwelleth in you?

I Corinthians 3:16

What? know ye not that your body is the temple of the Holy Ghost *which is* in you, which ye have of God, and ye are not your own?

For ye are bought with a price: therefore glorify God in your body, and in your spirit, which are God's.

I Corinthians 6:19,20

And I heard a great voice out of heaven saying, Behold, the tabernacle of God *is* with men, and he will dwell with them, and they shall be his people, and God himself shall be with them, *and be* their God.

Revelation 21:3

Neither shall they say, Lo here! or, lo there! for, behold, the kingdom of God is within you.

Luke 17:21

Behold, I stand at the door, and knock: if any man hear my voice, and open the door, I will come in to him, and will sup with him, and he with me.

Revelation 3:20

Now therefore ye are no more strangers and foreigners, but fellowcitizens with the saints, and of the household of God;

And are built upon the foundation of the apostles and prophets, Jesus Christ himself being the chief corner *stone*;

In whom all the building fitly framed together groweth unto an holy temple in the Lord:

In whom ye also are builded together for an habitation of God through the Spirit.

Ephesians 2:19-22

Jesus answered and said unto him, If a man love me, he will keep my words: and my Father will love him, and we will come unto him, and make our abode with him.

John 14:23

For though he was crucified through weakness, yet he liveth by the power of God. For we also are weak in him, but we shall live with him by the power of God toward you.

II Corinthians 13:4

That he might present it to himself a glorious church, not having spot, or wrinkle, or any such thing; but that it should be holy and without blemish.

Ephesians 5:27

Reveal His Glory

Who *is* this King of glory? The Lord strong and mighty, the Lord mighty in battle.

Lift up your heads, O ye gates; even lift *them* up, ye everlasting doors; and the King of glory shall come in.

Who is this King of glory? The Lord of hosts, he *is* the King of glory. Selah.

Psalm 24:8-10

Every valley shall be exalted, and every mountain and hill shall be made low: and the crooked shall be made straight, and the rough places plain:

And the glory of the Lord shall be revealed, and all flesh shall see *it* together: for the mouth of the Lord hath spoken *it*.

Isaiah 40:4,5

But as it is written, Eye hath not seen, nor ear heard, neither have entered into the heart of man, the things which God hath prepared for them that love him.

But God hath revealed *them* unto us by his Spirit: for the Spirit searcheth all things, yea, the deep things of God.

I Corinthians 2:9,10

The heavens declare the glory of God; and the firmament sheweth his handywork.

Psalm 19:1

Hearken unto this, O Job: stand still, and consider the wondrous works of God.

Job 37:14

How great *are* his signs! and how mighty *are* his wonders! his kingdom *is* an everlasting kingdom, and his dominion *is* from generation to generation.

Daniel 4:3

Arise, shine; for thy light is come, and the glory of the Lord is risen upon thee.
For, behold, the darkness shall cover the earth, and gross darkness the people: but the Lord shall arise upon thee, and his glory shall be seen upon thee.

Isaiah 60:1,2

And one cried unto another, and said, Holy, holy, holy, *is* the Lord of hosts: the whole earth *is* full of his glory.

Isaiah 6:3

Enter into the rock, and hide thee in the dust, for fear of the Lord, and for the glory of his majesty.

The lofty looks of man shall be humbled, and the haughtiness of men shall be bowed down, and the Lord alone shall be exalted in that day.

Isaiah 2:10,11

And the loftiness of man shall be bowed down, and the haughtiness of men shall be made low: and the Lord alone shall be exalted in that day.

And the idols he shall utterly abolish.

And they shall go into the holes of the rocks, and into the caves of the earth, for fear of the Lord, and for the glory of his majesty, when he ariseth to shake terribly the earth.

In that day a man shall cast his idols of silver, and his idols of gold, which they made *each one* for himself to worship, to the moles and to the bats;

To go into the clefts of the rocks, and into the tops of the ragged rocks, for fear of the Lord, and for the glory of his majesty, when he ariseth to shake terribly the earth.

Isaiah 2:17-21

For I reckon that the sufferings of this present time *are* not worthy *to be compared* with the glory which shall be revealed in us.

Romans 8:18

He loveth righteousness and judgment: the earth is full of the goodness of the Lord.

Psalm 33:5

Prepare A Heavenly Kingdom

For I am now ready to be offered, and the time of my departure is at hand.

I have fought a good fight, I have finished *my* course, I have kept the faith:

Henceforth there is laid up for me a crown of righteousness, which the Lord, the righteous judge, shall give me at that day: and not to me only, but unto all them also that love his appearing.

II Timothy 4:6-8

Blessed *are* they which are persecuted for righteousness' sake: for theirs is the kingdom of heaven.

Matthew 5:10

Whosoever therefore shall break one of these least commandments, and shall teach men so, he shall be called the least in the kingdom of heaven: but whosoever shall do and teach *them*, the same shall be called great in the kingdom of heaven.

Matthew 5:19

When the Son of man shall come in his glory, and all the holy angels with him, then shall he sit upon the throne of his glory:

And before him shall be gathered all nations: and he shall separate them one from another, as a shepherd divideth *his* sheep from the goats:

And he shall set the sheep on his right hand, but the goats on the left.

Then shall the King say unto them on his right hand, Come, ye blessed of my Father, inherit the kingdom prepared for you from the foundation of the world:

Matthew 25:31-34

If any man serve me, let him follow me; and where I am, there shall also my servant be: if any man serve me, him will *my* Father honour.

John 12:26

But lay up for yourselves treasures in heaven, where neither moth nor rust doth corrupt, and where thieves do not break through nor steal:

Matthew 6:20

The Lord knoweth the days of the upright: and their inheritance shall be for ever.

Psalm 37:18

Fear none of those things which thou shalt suffer: behold, the devil shall cast *some* of you into prison, that ye may be tried; and ye shall have tribulation ten days: be thou faithful unto death, and I will give thee a crown of life.

Revelation 2:10

Beloved, think it not strange concerning the fiery trial which is to try you, as though some strange thing happened unto you:

But rejoice, inasmuch as ye are partakers of Christ's sufferings; that, when his glory shall be revealed, ye may be glad also with exceeding joy.

I Peter 4:12,13

And when the chief Shepherd shall appear, ye shall receive a crown of glory that fadeth not away.

I Peter 5:4

Blessed *is* the man that endureth temptation: for when he is tried, he shall receive the crown of life, which the Lord hath promised to them that love him.

James 1:12

If we suffer, we shall also reign with *him:* if we deny *him*, he also will deny us:

II Timothy 2:12

But as it is written, Eye hath not seen, nor ear heard, neither have entered into the heart of man, the things which God hath prepared for them that love him.

I Corinthians 2:9

For whosoever shall give you a cup of water to drink in my name, because ye belong to Christ, verily I say unto you, he shall not lose his reward.

Mark 9:41

His Lord said unto him, Well done, *thou* good and faithful servant: thou hast been faithful over a few things, I will make thee ruler over many things: enter thou into the joy of the lord.

Matthew 25:21

We Are
Commanded
To Care For
Those Around
Us By...

Loving One Another

Let love be without dissimulation. Abhor that which is evil; cleave to that which is good.

Be kindly affectioned one to another with brotherly love; in honour preferring one another;

Romans 12:9,10

But as touching brotherly love ye need not that I write unto you: for ye yourselves are taught of God to love one another.

I Thessalonians 4:9

We are bound to thank God always for you, brethren, as it is meet, because that your faith groweth exceedingly, and the charity of every one of you all toward each other aboundeth;

So that we ourselves glory in you in the churches of God for your patience and faith in all your persecutions and tribulations that ye endure:

II Thessalonians 1:3,4

Master, which *is* the great commandment in the law?

Jesus said unto him, Thou shalt love the Lord thy God with all thy heart, and with all thy soul, and with all thy mind.

This is the first and great commandment.

And the second *is* like unto it, Thou shalt love thy neighbour as thyself.

On these two commandments hang all the law and the prophets.

Matthew 22:36-40

Beloved, let us love one another: for love is of God; and every one that loveth is born of God, and knoweth God.

He that loveth not knoweth not God; for God is love.

I John 4:7,8

We know that we have passed from death unto life, because we love the brethren. He that loveth not *his* brother abideth in death.

I John 3:14

Hereby perceive we the love *of God*, because he laid down his life for us: and we ought to lay down our lives for the brethren.

I John 3:16

Owe no man any thing, but to love one another: for he that loveth another hath fulfilled the law.

Romans 13:8

Love worketh no ill to his neighbor: therefore love *is* the fulfilling of the law.

Romans 13:10

Husbands, love your wives, even as Christ also loved the church, and gave himself for it:

Ephesians 5:25

So ought men to love their wives as their own bodies. He that loveth his wife loveth himself.

For no man ever yet hated his own flesh; but nourisheth and cherisheth it, even as the Lord the church:

Ephesians 5:28,29

For this cause shall a man leave his father and mother, and shall be joined unto his wife, and they two shall be one flesh.

This is a great mystery: but I speak concerning Christ and the church.

Nevertheless let every one of you in particular so love his wife even as himself; and the wife *see* that she reverence *her* husband.

Ephesians 5:31-33

For all the law is fulfilled in one word, *even* in this; Thou shalt love thy neighbor as thyself.

Galatians 5:14

Forgiving One Another

Behold, how good and how pleasant *it
is* for brethren to dwell together in unity!
Psalm 133:1

Ye have heard that it hath been said,
Thou shalt love thy neighbour, and hate
thine enemy.

But I say unto you, Love your enemies,
bless them that curse you, do good to them
that hate you, and pray for them which despitefully use you, and persecute you;
Matthew 5:43,44

And forgive us our debts, as we forgive
our debtors.

And lead us not into temptation, but
deliver us from evil: For thine is the kingdom, and the power, and the glory, for ever.
Amen.

For if ye forgive men their trespasses,
your heavenly Father will also forgive you:

But if ye forgive not men their trespasses, neither will your Father forgive your
trespasses.

Matthew 6:12-15

Therefore if thou bring thy gift to the altar, and there rememberest that thy brother hath ought against thee:

Leave there thy gift before the altar, and go thy way; first be reconciled to thy brother, and then come and offer thy gift.

Matthew 5:23,24

Then came Peter to him, said, Lord, how oft shall my brother sin against me, and I forgive him? till seven times?

Jesus saith unto him, I say not unto thee, Until seven times: but, Until seventy times seven.

Matthew 18:21,22

Be ye angry, and sin not: let not the sun go down upon your wrath:

Neither give place to the devil.

Ephesians 4:26,27

Let all bitterness, and wrath, and anger, and clamour, and evil speaking, be put away from you, with all malice:

And be ye kind one to another, tenderhearted, forgiving one another, even as God for Christ's sake hath forgiven you.

Ephesians 4:31,32

If it be possible, as much as lieth in you, live peaceably with all men.

Dearly beloved, avenge not yourselves, but *rather* give place unto wrath: for it is written, Vengeance *is* mine; I will repay, saith the Lord.

Therefore if thine enemy hunger, feed him; if he thirst, give him drink: for in so doing thou shalt heap coals of fire on his head.

Be not overcome of evil, but overcome evil with good.

Romans 12:18-21

Ye have heard that it hath been said, An eye for an eye, and a tooth for a tooth:

But I say unto you, That ye resist not evil: but whosoever shall smite thee on thy right cheek, turn to him the other also.

And if any man will sue thee at the law, and take away thy coat, let him have *thy* cloak also.

And whosoever shall compel thee to go a mile, go with him twain.

Give to him that asketh thee, and from him that would borrow of thee turn not thou away.

Matthew 5:38-42

I Therefore, the prisoner of the Lord, beseech you that ye walk worthy of the vocation wherewith ye are called.

With all lowliness and meekness, with longsuffering, forbearing one another in love;

Endeavouring to keep the unity of the Spirit in the bond of peace.

Ephesians 4:1-3

Moreover if thy brother shall trespass against thee, go and tell him his fault between thee and him alone: if he shall hear thee, thou hast gained thy brother.

But if he will not hear *thee, then* take with thee one or two more, that in the mouth of two or three witnesses every word may be established.

Matthew 18:15,16

Brethren, if a man be overtaken in a fault, ye which are spiritual, restore such an one in the spirit of meekness; considering thyself, lest thou also be tempted.

Galatians 6:1

WE ARE COMMANDED TO CARE
FOR THOSE AROUND US BY...

Praying For One Another

Confess *your* faults one to another, and pray one for another, that ye may be healed. The effectual fervent prayer of a righteous man availeth much.

James 5:16

Again I say unto you, That if two of you shall agree on earth as touching any thing that they shall ask, it shall be done for them of my Father which is in heaven.

For where two or three are gathered together in my name, there am I in the midst of them.

Matthew 18:19,20

Now I beseech you, brethren, for the Lord Jesus Christ's sake, and for the love of the Spirit, that ye strive together with me in *your* prayers to God for me;

Romans 15:30

Finally, brethren, pray for us, that the word of the Lord may have *free* course, and be glorified, even as *it is* with you:

And that we may be delivered from unreasonable and wicked men: for all *men* have not faith.

II Thessalonians 3:1,2

We give thanks to God always for you all, making mention of you in our prayers;

Remembering without ceasing your work of faith, and labour of love, and patience of hope in our Lord Jesus Christ, in the sight of God and our Father;

I Thessalonians 1:2,3

Let us therefore come boldly unto the throne of grace, that we may obtain mercy, and find grace to help in time of need.

Hebrews 4:16

For this cause we also, since the day we heard *it,* do not cease to pray for you, and to desire that ye might be filled with the knowledge of his will in all wisdom and spiritual understanding;

That ye might walk worthy of the Lord unto all pleasing, being fruitful in every good work, and increasing in the knowledge of God;

Colossians 1:9,10

We give thanks to God and the Father of our Lord Jesus Christ, praying always for you,

Colossians 1:3

Ye also helping together by prayer for us, that for the gift *bestowed* upon us by the means of many persons thanks may be given by many on our behalf.

II Corinthians 1:11

Peter therefore was kept in prison: but prayer was made without ceasing of the church unto God for him.

Acts 12:5

Wherefore I also, after I heard of your faith in the Lord Jesus, and love unto all the saints,

Cease not to give thanks for you, making mention of you in my prayers;

Ephesians 1:15,16

I exhort therefore, that, first of all, supplications, prayers, intercessions, *and* giving of thanks, be made for all men;

For kings, and *for* all that are in authority; that we may lead a quiet and peaceable life in all godliness and honesty.

For this *is* good and acceptable in the sight of God our Saviour;

Who will have all men to be saved, and to come unto the knowledge of the truth.

I Timothy 2:1-4

Rejoicing With One Another

But let all those that put their trust in thee rejoice: let them ever shout for joy, because thou defendest them: let them also that love thy name be joyful in thee.

For thou, Lord, wilt bless the righteous; with favour wilt thou compass him as *with* a shield.

Psalm 5:11,12

Heaviness in the heart of man maketh it stoop: but a good word maketh it glad.

Proverbs 12:25

Rejoice with them that do rejoice, and weep with them that weep.

Romans 12:15

And thou shalt rejoice in every good *thing* which the Lord thy God hath given unto thee, and unto thine house, thou, and the Levite, and the stranger that *is* among you.

Deuteronomy 26:11

Let all those that seek thee rejoice and be glad in thee: let such as love thy salvation say continually, The Lord be magnified.

Psalm 40:16

O Clap your hands, all ye people; shout unto God with the voice of triumph.

Psalm 47:1

I will also clothe her priests with salvation: and her saints shall shout aloud for joy.

Psalm 132:16

For what *is* our hope, or joy, or crown of rejoicing? *Are* not even ye in the presence of our Lord Jesus Christ at his coming?

For ye are our glory and joy.

I Thessalonians 2:19,20

Yea, and if I be offered upon the sacrifice and service of your faith, I joy, and rejoice with you all.

For the same cause also do ye joy, and rejoice with me.

Philippians 2:17,18

And he that reapeth receiveth wages, and gathereth fruit unto life eternal: that both he that soweth and he that reapeth may rejoice together.

John 4:36

But I determined this with myself, that I would not come again to you in heaviness.

For if I make you sorry, who is he then that maketh me glad, but the same which is made sorry by me?

And I wrote this same unto you, lest, when I came, I should have sorrow from them of whom I ought to rejoice; having confidence in you all, that my joy is *the joy* of you all.

II Corinthians 2:1-3

Exhorting One Another

Ye *are* witnesses, and God *also*, how holily and justly and unblameably we behaved ourselves among you that believe:

As ye know how we exhorted and comforted and charged every one of you, as a father *doth* his children,

I Thessalonians 2:10,11

Let no corrupt communication proceed out of your mouth, but that which is good to the use of edifying, that it may minister grace unto the hearers.

Ephesians 4:29

But exhort one another daily, while it is called To day; lest any of you be hardened through the deceitfulness of sin.

Hebrews 3:13

Young men likewise exhort to be sober minded.

In all things shewing thyself a pattern of good works: in doctrine *shewing* uncorruptness, gravity, sincerity,

Sound speech, that cannot be condemned; that he that is of the contrary part may be ashamed, having no evil thing to say of you.

Titus 2:6-8

Preach the word; be instant in season, out of season; reprove, rebuke, exhort with all longsuffering and doctrine.

II Timothy 4:2

Confess *your* faults one to another, and pray one for another, that ye may be healed. The effectual fervent prayer of a righteous man availeth much.

James 5:16

Look not every man on his own things, but every man also on the things of others.

Philippians 2:4

Wherefore comfort yourselves together, and edify one another, even as also ye do.

I Thessalonians 5:11

For, brethren, ye have been called unto liberty; only *use* not liberty for an occasion to the flesh, but by love serve one another.

Galatians 5:13

Till I come, give attendance to reading, to exhortation, to doctrine.

I Timothy 4:13

Preach the word; be instant in season, out of season; reprove, rebuke, exhort with all longsuffering and doctrine.

II Timothy 4:2

Furthermore then we beseech you, brethren, and exhort *you* by the Lord Jesus, that as ye have received of us how ye ought to walk and to please God, *so* ye would abound more and more.

I Thessalonians 4:1

Now the God of peace, that brought again from the dead our Lord Jesus, that great shepherd of the sheep, through the blood of the everlasting convenant,

Make you perfect in every good work to do his will, working in you that which is wellpleasing in his sight, through Jesus Christ; to whom *be* glory for ever and ever. Amen.

And I beseech you, brethren, suffer the word of exhortation: for I have written a letter unto you in few words.

Hebrews 13:20-22

And let us consider one another to provoke unto love and to good works:

Not forsaking the assembling of ourselves together, as the manner of some *is*; but exhorting *one another*: and so much the more, as ye see the day approaching.

Hebrews 10:24,25

The elders which are among you I exhort, who am also an elder, and a witness of the sufferings of Christ, and also a partaker of the glory that shall be revealed:

Feed the flock of God which is among you, taking the oversight *thereof*, not by constraint, but willingly; not for filthy lucre, but of a ready mind;

Neither as being lords over *God's* heritage, but being ensamples to the flock.

I Peter 5:1-3

Building Faith
In One Another

As ye have therefore received Christ Jesus the Lord, *so* walk ye in him:

Rooted and built up in him, and stablished in the faith, as ye have been taught, abounding therein with thanksgiving.

Colossians 2:6,7

That Christ may dwell in your hearts by faith; that ye, being rooted and grounded in love,

May be able to comprehend with all saints what *is* the breadth, and length, and depth, and height;

And to know the love of Christ, which passeth knowledge, that ye might be filled with all the fulness of God.

Ephesians 3:17-19

And I, brethren, when I came to you, came not with excellency of speech or of wisdom, declaring unto you the testimony of God.

For I determined not to know any thing among you, save Jesus Christ, and him crucified.

And I was with you in weakness, and in fear, and in much trembling.

And my speech and my preaching *was* not with enticing words of man's wisdom, but in demonstration of the spirit and of power:

That your faith should not stand in the wisdom of men, but in the power of God.

I Corinthians 2:1-5

But we were gentle among you, even as a nurse cherisheth her children:

So being affectionately desirous of you, we were willing to have imparted unto you, not the gospel of God only, but also our own souls, because ye were dear unto us.

For ye remember, brethren, our labour and travail: for labouring night and day, because we would not be chargeable unto any of you, we preached unto you the gospel of God.

I Thessalonians 2:7-9

Beloved, when I gave all diligence to write unto you of the common salvation, it was needful for me to write unto you, and exhort *you* that ye should earnestly contend for the faith which was once delivered unto the saints.

Jude 3

But ye, beloved, building up yourselves on your most holy faith, praying in the Holy Ghost,

Keep yourselves in the love of God, looking for the mercy of our Lord Jesus Christ unto eternal life.

Jude 20,21

But sanctify the Lord God in your hearts: and *be* ready always to *give* an answer to every man that asketh you a reason of the hope that is in you with meekness and fear:

I Peter 3:15

Holding fast the faithful word as he hath been taught, that he may be able by sound doctrine both to exhort and to convince the gainsayers.

Titus 1:9

If thou put the brethren in remembrance of these things, thou shalt be a good minister of Jesus Christ, nourished up in the words of faith and of good doctrine, whereunto thou hast attained.

I Timothy 4:6

Let your speech *be* alway with grace, seasoned with salt, that ye may know how ye ought to answer every man.

Colossians 4:6

Let him that is taught in the word communicate unto him that teacheth in all good things.

Galatians 6:6

Let us therefore follow after the things which make for peace, and things wherewith one may edify another.

Romans 14:19

And let us consider one another to provoke unto love and to good works:

Hebrews 10:24

For I say, through the grace given unto me, to every man that is among you, not to think *of himself* more highly than he ought to think; but to think soberly, according as God hath dealt to every man the measure of faith.

Romans 12:3

For what thanks can we render to God again for you, for all the joy wherewith we joy for your sakes before our God;

Night and day praying exceedingly that we might see your face, and might perfect that which is lacking in your faith?

I Thessalonians 3:9,10

Expecting The Best
From One Another

As every man hath received the gift, *even so* minister the same one to another, as good stewards of the manifold grace of God.

I Peter 4:10

From whom the whole body fitly joined together and compacted by that which every joint supplieth, according to the effectual working in the measure of every part, maketh increase of the body unto the edifying of itself in love.

Ephesians 4:16

Now he that ministereth seed to the sower both minister bread for *your* food, and multiply your seed sown, and increase the fruits of your righteousness;

II Corinthians 9:10

To whom God would make known what *is* the riches of the glory of this mystery among the Gentiles; which is Christ in you, the hope of glory:

Whom we preach, warning every man, and teaching every man in all wisdom; that we may present every man perfect in Christ Jesus:

Colossians 1:27,28

Finally, *be ye* all of one mind, having compassion one of another, love as brethren, *be* pitiful, *be* courteous:

Not rendering evil for evil, or railing for railing: but contrariwise blessing; knowing that ye are thereunto called, that ye should inherit a blessing.

I Peter 3:8,9

For ye are yet carnal: for whereas *there is* among you envying, and strife, and divisions, are ye not carnal, and walk as men?

For while one saith, I am of Paul; and another, I *am* of Apollos; are ye not carnal?

Who then is Paul, and who *is* Apollos, but ministers by whom ye believed, even as the Lord gave to every man?

I have planted, Apollos watered; but God gave the increase.

So then neither is he that planteth any thing, neither he that watereth; but God that giveth the increase.

Now he that planteth and he that watereth are one: and every man shall receive his own reward according to his own labour.

For we are labourers together with God: ye are God's husbandry, *ye are* God's building.

I Corinthians 3:3-9

If we live in the Spirit, let us also walk in the Spirit.

Galatians 5:25

For the body is not one member, but many.

If the foot shall say, Because I am not the hand, I am not of the body; is it therefore not of the body?

And if the ear shall say, Because I am not the eye, I am not of the body; is it therefore not of the body?

If the whole body *were* an eye, where *were* the hearing? If the whole *were* hearing, where *were* the smelling?

But now hath God set the members every one of them in the body, as it hath pleased him.

And if they were all one member, where *were* the body?

But now *are they* many members, yet but one body.

And the eye cannot say unto the hand, I have no need of thee: nor again the head to the feet, I have no need of you.

Nay, much more those members of the body, which seem to be more feeble, are necessary:

And those *members* of the body, which we think to be less honourable, upon these we bestow more abundant honour; and our uncomely *parts* have more abundant comeliness.

For our comely *parts* have no need: but God hath tempered the body together, having given more abundant honour to that *part* which lacked.

I Corinthians 12:14-24

Judge not, that ye be not judged.

For with what judgment ye judge, ye shall be judged: and with what measure ye mete, it shall be measured to you again.

And why beholdest thou the mote that is in thy brother's eye, but considerest not the beam that is in thine own eye?

Or how wilt thou say to thy brother, Let me pull out the mote out of thine eye; and, behold, a beam *is* in thine own eye?

Thou hypocrite, first cast out the beam out of thine own eye; and then shalt thou see clearly to cast out the mote out of thy brother's eye.

Matthew 7:1-5

Being Kind To One Another

A Soft answer turneth away wrath: but grievous words stir up anger.

Proverbs 15:1

Let all your things be done with charity.

I Corinthians 16:14

Walk in wisdom toward them that are without, redeeming the time.

Let your speech *be* alway with grace, seasoned with salt, that ye may know how ye ought to answer every man.

Colossians 4:5,6

Wherefore, my beloved brethren, let every man be swift to hear, slow to speak, slow to wrath:

For the wrath of man worketh not the righteousness of God.

James 1:19,20

Even so the tongue is a little member, and boasteth great things. Behold, how great a matter a little fire kindleth!

James 3:5

Hearken, my beloved brethren, Hath not God chosen the poor of this world rich in faith, and heirs of the kingdom which he hath promised to them that love him?

James 2:5

If ye fulfil the royal law according to the scripture, Thou shalt love thy neighbour as thyself, ye do well:

James 2:8

Finally, brethren, farewell. Be perfect, be of good comfort, be of one mind, live in peace; and the God of love and peace shall be with you.
Greet one another with an holy kiss.
All the saints salute you.
The grace of the Lord Jesus Christ, and the love of God, and the communion of the Holy Ghost, *be* with you all. Amen.

II Corinthians 13:11-14

And be ye kind one to another, tender-hearted, forgiving one another, even as God for Christ's sake hath forgiven you.

Ephesians 4:32

Thus speaketh the Lord of hosts, saying, Execute true judgment, and shew mercy and compassions every man to his brother:

Zechariah 7:9

And if ye do good to them which do good to you, what thank have ye? for sinners also do even the same.

And if ye lend *to them* of whom ye hope to receive, what thank have ye? for sinners also lend to sinners, to receive as much again.

But love ye your enemies, and do good, and lend, hoping for nothing again; and your reward shall be great, and ye shall be the children of the Highest: for he is kind unto the unthankful and *to* the evil.

Luke 6:33-35

And David said, Is there yet any that is left of the house of Saul, that I may shew him kindness for Jonathan's sake?

And *there was* of the house of Saul a servant whose name *was* Ziba. And when they had called him unto David, the king said unto him, *Art* thou Ziba? And he said, Thy servant *is he*.

And the king said, *Is* there not yet any of the house of Saul, that I may shew the kindness of God unto him? And Ziba said unto the king, Jonathan hath yet a son, *which is* lame on *his* feet.

II Samuel 9:1-3

Now when Mephibosheth, the son of Jonathan, the son of Saul, was come unto David, he fell on his face, and did reverence. And David said, Mephibosheth. And he answered, Behold thy servant!

And David said unto him, Fear not: for I will surely shew thee kindness for Jonathan thy father's sake, and will restore thee all the land of Saul thy father; and thou shalt eat bread at my table continually.

II Samuel 9:6,7

Submitting To Each Other

But Jesus called them *unto him*, and said, Ye know that the princes of the Gentiles exercise dominion over them, and they that are great exercise authority upon them.

But it shall not be so among you: but whosoever will be great among you, let him be your minister;

And whosoever will be chief among you, let him be your servant:

Even as the Son of man came not to be ministered unto, but to minister, and to give his life a ransom for many.

Matthew 20:25-28

Likewise, ye younger, submit yourselves unto the elder. Yea, all *of you* be subject one to another, and be clothed with humility: for God resisteth the proud, and giveth grace to the humble.

Humble yourselves therefore under the mighty hand of God, that he may exalt you in due time:

I Peter 5:5,6

Obey them that have the rule over you, and submit yourselves: for they watch for your souls, as they that must give account, that they may do it with joy, and not with grief: for that *is* unprofitable for you.

Hebrews 13:17

If *there be* therefore any consolation in Christ, if any comfort of love, if any fellowship of the Spirit, if any bowels and mercies,

Fulfil ye my joy, that ye be likeminded, having the same love, *being* of one accord, of one mind.

Let nothing *be done* through strife or vainglory; but in lowliness of mind let each esteem other better than themselves.

Philippians 2:1-3

Giving thanks always for all things unto God and the Father in the name of our Lord Jesus Christ;

Submitting yourselves one to another in the fear of God.

Ephesians 5:20,21

For though I be free from all *men*, yet have I made myself servant unto all, that I might gain the more.

I Corinthians 9:19

We then that are strong ought to bear the infirmities of the weak, and not to please ourselves.

Let every one of us please *his* neighbour for *his* good to edification.

For even Christ pleased not himself; but, as it is written, The reproaches of them that reproached thee fell on me.

Romans 15:1-3

Wives, submit yourselves unto your own husbands, as it is fit in the Lord.

Husbands, love *your* wives, and be not bitter against them.

Children, obey *your* parents in all things: for this is well pleasing unto the Lord.

Fathers, provoke not your children *to anger*, lest they be discouraged.

Colossians 3:18-21

God *is* faithful, by whom ye were called unto the fellowship of his Son Jesus Christ our Lord.

Now I beseech you, brethren, by the name of our Lord Jesus Christ, that ye all speak the same thing, and *that* there be no divisions among you; but *that* ye be perfectly joined together in the same mind and in the same judgment.

I Corinthians 1:9,10

Submit yourselves to every ordinance of man for the Lord's sake: whether it be to the king, as supreme;

Or unto governors, as unto them that are sent by him for the punishment of evildoers, and for the praise of them that do well.

I Peter 2:13,14

Remember them which have the rule over you, who have spoken unto you the word of God: whose faith follow, considering the end of *their* conversation.

Hebrews 13:7

**WE ARE COMMANDED TO CARE
FOR THOSE AROUND US BY...**

Bearing One
Another's Burdens

Bear ye one another's burdens, and so fulfil the law of Christ.

Galatians 6:2

They helped every one his neighbour; and *every one* said to his brother, Be of good courage.

Isaiah 41:6

Peter therefore was kept in prison: but prayer was made without ceasing of the church unto God for him.

Acts 12:5

For none of us liveth to himself, and no man dieth to himself.

Romans 14:7

Now I beseech you, brethren, for the Lord Jesus Christ's sake, and for the love of the Spirit, that ye strive together with me in *your* prayers to God for me;

That I may be delivered from them that do not believe in Judaea; and that my service which *I have* for Jerusalem may be accepted of the saints;

That I may come unto you with joy by the will of God, and may with you be refreshed.

Now the God of peace *be* with you all. Amen.

Romans 15:30-33

And whether one member suffer, all the members suffer with it; or one member be honoured, all the members rejoice with it.

I Corinthians 12:26

Who comforteth us in all our tribulation, that we may be able to comfort them which are in any trouble, by the comfort wherewith we ourselves are comforted of God.

For as the sufferings of Christ abound in us, so our consolation also aboundeth by Christ.

And whether we be afflicted, *it is* for your consolation and salvation, which is effectual in the enduring of the same sufferings which we also suffer: or whether we be comforted, *it is* for your consolation and salvation.

And our hope of you *is* stedfast, knowing, that as ye are partakers of the sufferings, so *shall ye be* also of the consolation.

II Corinthians 1:4-7

Let brotherly love continue.

Be not forgetful to entertain strangers: for thereby some have entertained angels unawares.

Remember them that are in bonds, as bound with them; *and* them which suffer adversity, as being yourselves also in the body.

Hebrews 13:1-3

Be careful for nothing; but in every thing by prayer and supplication with thanksgiving let your requests be made known unto God.

And the peace of God, which passeth all understanding, shall keep your hearts and minds through Christ Jesus.

Philippians 4:6,7

Pure religion and undefiled before God and the Father is this, To visit the fatherless and widows in their affliction, *and* to keep himself unspotted from the world.

James 1:27

And *if* thou draw out thy soul to the hungry, and satisfy the afflicted soul; then shall thy light rise in obscurity, and thy darkness *be* as the noonday:

Isaiah 58:10

Showing Mercy To Others

For the poor shall never cease out of the land: therefore I command thee, saying, Thou shalt open thine hand wide unto thy brother, to thy poor, and to thy needy, in thy land.

Deuteronomy 15:11

And it shall be, if thou go with us, yea, it shall be, that what goodness the Lord shall do unto us, the same will we do unto thee.

Numbers 10:32

Every man *shall give* as he is able, according to the blessing of the Lord thy God which he hath given thee.

Deuteronomy 16:17

Hear me when I call, O God of my righteousness: thou hast enlarged me *when I was* in distress; have mercy upon me, and hear my prayer.

Psalms 4:1

And the word of the Lord came unto Zechariah, saying,

Thus speaketh the Lord of hosts, saying, Execute true judgment, and shew mercy and compassions every man to his brother:

Zechariah 7:8,9

And Jesus went forth, and saw a great multitude, and was moved with compassion toward them, and he healed their sick.

And when it was evening, his disciples came to him, saying, This is a desert place, and the time is now past; send the multitude away, that they may go into the villages, and buy themselves victuals.

But Jesus said unto them, They need not depart; give ye them to eat.

Matthew 14:14-16

For I was an hungred, and ye gave me meat: I was thirsty, and ye gave me drink: I was a stranger, and ye took me in:

Naked, and ye clothed me: I was sick, and ye visited me: I was in prison, and ye came unto me.

Then shall the righteous answer him, saying, Lord, when saw we thee an hungred, and fed *thee*? or thirsty, and gave *thee* drink?

When saw we thee a stranger, and took *thee* in? or naked, and clothed *thee*?

Or when saw we thee sick, or in prison, and came unto thee?

And the King shall answer and say unto them, Verily I say unto you, Inasmuch as ye have done *it* unto one of the least of these my brethren, ye have done *it* unto me.

Matthew 25:35-40

And the people asked him, saying, What shall we do then?

He answereth and saith unto them, He that hath two coats, let him impart to him that hath none; and he that hath meat, let him do likewise.

Luke 3:10,11

And let us not be weary in well doing: for in due season we shall reap, if we faint not.

As we have therefore opportunity, let us do good unto all *men*, especially unto them who are of the household of faith.

Galatians 6:9,10

If a brother or sister be naked, and destitute of daily food,

And one of you say unto them, Depart in peace, be *ye* warmed and filled; notwithstanding ye give them not those things which are needful to the body; what *doth it* profit?

James 2:15,16

Hereby perceive we the love of God, because he laid down his life for us: and we ought to lay down our lives for the brethren.

I John 3:16

Defend the poor and fatherless: do justice to the afflicted and needy.

Deliver the poor and needy: rid *them* out of the hand of the wicked.

Psalm 82:3,4

Honouring The Name Of The Lord Together

I will bless the Lord at all times: his praise *shall* continually *be* in my mouth.

My soul shall make her boast in the Lord: the humble shall hear *thereof*, and be glad.

O magnify the Lord with me, and let us exalt his name together.

Psalm 34:1-3

Sing unto the Lord, O ye saints of his, and give thanks at the remembrance of his holiness.

Psalm 30:4

I will make thy name to be remembered in all generations: therefore shall the people praise thee for ever and ever.

Psalm 45:17

In God we boast all the day long, and praise thy name for ever. Selah.

Psalm 44:8

Make a joyful noise unto God, all ye lands:

Psalm 66:1

But I will declare for ever; I will sing praises to the God of Jacob.

Psalm 75:9

Rejoice in the Lord, ye righteous; and give thanks at the remembrance of his holiness.

Psalm 97:12

It is a good *thing* to give thanks unto the Lord, and to sing praises unto thy name, O most High:
To shew forth thy lovingkindness in the morning, and thy faithfulness every night,

Psalm 92:1,2

O Give thanks unto the Lord; call upon his name: make known his deeds among the people.
Sing unto him, sing psalms unto him: talk ye of all his wondrous works.
Glory ye in his holy name: let the heart of them rejoice that seek the Lord.
Seek the Lord, and his strength: seek his face evermore.
Remember his marvellous works that he hath done; his wonders, and the judgments of his mouth;

Psalm 105:1-5

Wherefore also we pray always for you, that our God would count you worthy of *this* calling, and fulfil all the good pleasure of *his* goodness, and the work of faith with power:

That the name of our Lord Jesus Christ may be glorified in you, and ye in him, according to the grace of our God and the Lord Jesus Christ.

II Thessalonians 1:11,12

Those things, which ye have both learned, and received, and heard, and seen in me, do: and the God of peace shall be with you.

Philippians 4:9

I thank my God, making mention of thee always in my prayers,

Hearing of thy love and faith, which thou hast toward the Lord Jesus, and toward all saints;

That the communication of thy faith may become effectual by the acknowledging of every good thing which is in you in Christ Jesus.

For we have great joy and consolation in thy love, because the bowels of the saints are refreshed by thee, brother.

Philemon 1:4-7

By this we know that we love the children of God, when we love God, and keep his commandments.

For this is the love of God, that we keep his commandments: and his commandments are not grievous.

For whatsoever is born of God overcometh the world: and this is the victory that overcometh the world, *even* our faith.

I John 5:2-4

Encouraging One Another's Spiritual Gifts

As every man hath received the gift, *even so* minister the same one to another, as good stewards of the manifold grace of God.

If any man speak, *let him speak* as the oracles of God; if any man minister, *let him do it* as of the ability which God giveth: that God in all things may be glorified through Jesus Christ, to whom be praise and dominion for ever and ever. Amen.

I Peter 4:10,11

For as we have many members in one body, and all members have not the same office:

So we, *being* many, are one body in Christ, and every one members one of another.

Having then gifts differing according to the grace that is given to us, whether prophecy, *let us prophesy* according to the proportion of faith;

Or ministry, *let us wait* on *our* ministering: or he that teacheth, on teaching;

Or he that exhorteth, on exhortation: he that giveth, *let him do it* with simplicity; he that ruleth, with diligence; he that sheweth mercy, with cheerfulness.

Let love be without dissimulation. Abhor that which is evil; cleave to that which is good.

Be kindly affectioned one to another with brotherly love; in honour preferring one another;

Not slothful in business; fervent in spirit; serving the Lord;

Romans 12:4-11

Even so ye, forasmuch as ye are zealous of spiritual *gifts*, seek that ye may excel to the edifying of the church.

I Corinthians 14:12

Wherefore I put thee in remembrance that thou stir up the gift of God, which is in thee by the putting on of my hands.

II Timothy 1:6

Let no corrupt communication proceed out of your mouth, but that which is good to the use of edifying, that it may minister grace unto the hearers.

Ephesians 4:29

For I long to see you, that I may impart unto you some spiritual gift, to the end ye may be established;

Romans 1:11

Neglect not the gift that is in thee, which was given thee by prophecy, with the laying on of the hands of the presbytery.

I Timothy 4:14

Let every one of us please *his* neighbour for *his* good to edification.

Romans 15:2

Now there are diversities of gifts, but the same Spirit.

And there are differences of administrations, but the same Lord.

And there are diversities of operations, but it is the same God which worketh all in all.

But the manifestation of the Spirit is given to every man to profit withal.

I Corinthians 12:4-7

For he that speaketh in an *unknown* tongue speaketh not unto men, but unto God: for no man understandeth *him*; howbeit in the spirit he speaketh mysteries.

But he that prophesieth speaketh unto men *to* edification, and exhortation, and comfort.

He that speaketh in an *unknown* tongue edifieth himself; but he that prophesieth edifieth the church.

I Corinthians 14:2-4

So likewise ye, except ye utter by the tongue words easy to be understood, how shall it be known what is spoken? for ye shall speak into the air.

There are, it may be, so many kinds of voices in the world, and none of them *is* without signification.

Therefore if I know not the meaning of the voice, I shall be unto him that speaketh a barbarian, and he that speaketh *shall be* a barbarian unto me.

Even so ye, forasmuch as ye are zealous of spiritual *gifts,* seek that ye may excel to the edifying of the church.

I Corinthians 14:9-12

Encouraging Fellowship And Worship

But if we walk in the light, as he is in the light, we have fellowship one with another, and the blood of Jesus Christ his Son cleanseth us from all sin.

I John 1:7

Let all those that seek thee rejoice and be glad in thee: and let such as love thy salvation say continually, Let God by magnified.

Psalms 70:4

Exalt ye the Lord our God, and worship at his footstool; *for* he *is* holy.

Psalm 99:5

The cup of blessing which we bless, is it not the communion of the blood of Christ? The bread which we break, is it not the communion of the body of Christ?

For we *being* many are one bread, *and* one body: for we are all partakers of that one bread.

I Corinthians 10:16,17

For where two or three are gathered together in my name, there am I in the midst of them.

Matthew 18:20

Now therefore ye are no more strangers and foreigners, but fellowcitizens with the saints, and of the household of God;

And are built upon the foundation of the apostles and prophets, Jesus Christ himself being the chief corner *stone*;

In whom all the building fitly framed together groweth unto an holy temple in the Lord:

In whom ye also are builded together for an habitation of God through the Spirit.

Ephesians 2:19-22

Let us hold fast the profession of *our* faith without wavering; (for he *is* faithful that promised;)

And let us consider one another to provoke unto love and to good works:

Not forsaking the assembling of ourselves together, as the manner of some *is;* but exhorting *one another*: and so much the more, as ye see the day approaching.

Hebrews 10:23-25

That which we have seen and heard declare we unto you, that ye also may have fellowship with us: and truly our fellowship *is* with the Father, and with his Son Jesus Christ.

And these things write we unto you, that your joy may be full.

I John 1:3,4

Wherefore comfort yourselves together, and edify one another, even as also ye do.

I Thessalonians 5:11

And they continued stedfastly in the apostles' doctrine and fellowship, and in breaking of bread, and in prayers.

Acts 2:42

Now the God of patience and consolation grant you to be likeminded one toward another according to Christ Jesus:

That ye may with one mind *and* one mouth glorify God, even the Father of our Lord Jesus Christ.

Romans 15:5,6

And the Lord make you to increase and abound in love one toward another, and toward all *men*, even as we *do* toward you:

I Thessalonians 3:12

Two *are* better than one; because they have a good reward for their labour.

For if they fall, the one will lift up his fellow: but woe to him *that is* alone when he falleth; for *he hath* not another to help him up.

Ecclesiastes 4:9,10

If *there be* therefore any consolation in Christ, if any comfort of love, if any fellowship of the Spirit, if any bowels and mercies,

Fulfil ye my joy, that ye be likeminded, having the same love, *being* of one accord, of one mind.

Philippians 2:1,2

Ye also, as lively stones, are built up a spiritual house, an holy priesthood, to offer up spiritual sacrifices, acceptable to God by Jesus Christ.

I Peter 2:5

But ye *are* a chosen generation, a royal priesthood, an holy nation, a peculiar people; that ye should shew forth the praises of him who hath called you out of darkness into his marvellous light;

I Peter 2:9

Guiding Others To The Truth

Go ye therefore, and teach all nations, baptizing them in the name of the Father, and of the Son, and of the Holy Ghost:

Teaching them to observe all things whatsoever I have commanded you: and, lo, I am with you alway, *even* unto the end of the world. Amen.

Matthew 28:19,20

Whosoever therefore shall confess me before men, him will I confess also before my Father which is in heaven.

Matthew 10:32

For I am not ashamed of the gospel of Christ: for it is the power of God unto salvation to every one that believeth; to the Jew first, and also to the Greek.

Romans 1:16

Ye are the light of the world. A city that is set on an hill cannot be hid.

Neither do men light a candle, and put it under a bushel, but on a candlestick; and it giveth light unto all that are in the house.

Let your light so shine before men, that they may see your good works, and glorify your Father which is in heaven.

Matthew 5:14-16

Brethren, if any of you do err from the truth, and one convert him;

Let him know, that he which converteth the sinner from the error of his way shall save a soul from death, and shall hide a multitude of sins.

James 5:19,20

For every tree is known by his own fruit. For of thorns men do not gather figs, nor of a bramble bush gather they grapes.

Luke 6:44

A good man out of the good treasure of his heart bringeth forth that which is good; and an evil man out of the evil treasure of his heart bringeth forth that which is evil: for of the abundance of the heart his mouth speaketh.

Luke 6:45

Howbeit Jesus suffered him not, but saith unto him, Go home to thy friends, and tell them how great things the Lord hath done for thee, and hath had compassion on thee.

Mark 5:19

I will sing of the mercies of the Lord for ever: with my mouth will I make known thy faithfulness to all generations.

Psalm 89:1

One generation shall praise thy works to another, and shall declare thy mighty acts.

Psalm 145:4

Then saith he unto his disciples, The harvest truly *is* plenteous, but the labourers *are* few;

Pray ye therefore the Lord of the harvest, that he will send forth labourers into his harvest.

Matthew 9:37,38

O sing unto the Lord a new song: sing unto the Lord, all the earth.

Sing unto the Lord, bless his name; shew forth his salvation from day to day.

Declare his glory among the heathen, his wonders among all people.

Psalm 96:1-3

I charge *thee* therefore before God, and the Lord Jesus Christ, who shall judge the quick and the dead at his appearing and his kingdom;

Preach the word; be instant in season, out of season; reprove, rebuke, exhort with all longsuffering and doctrine.

II Timothy 4:1,2

Helping Those Who Are Tempted

Let us not therefore judge one another any more: but judge this rather, that no man put a stumbling block or an occasion to fall in *his* brother's way.

I know, and am persuaded by the Lord Jesus, that *there is* nothing unclean of itself: but to him that esteemeth any thing to be unclean, to him *it is* unclean.

But if thy brother be grieved with *thy* meat, now walkest thou not charitably. Destroy not him with thy meat, for whom Christ died.

Romans 14:13-15

Wherefore, if meat make my brother to offend, I will eat no flesh while the world standeth, lest I make my brother to offend.

I Corinthians 8:13

And the servant of the Lord must not strive; but be gentle unto all *men*, apt to teach, patient,

In meekness instructing those that oppose themselves; if God peradventure will give them repentance to the acknowledging of the truth;

And *that* they may recover themselves out of the snare of the devil, who are taken captive by him at his will.

II Timothy 2:24-26

Who comforteth us in all our tribulation, that we may be able to comfort them which are in any trouble, by the comfort wherewith we ourselves are comforted of God.

II Corinthians 1:4

Remember them that are in bonds, as bound with them; *and* them which suffer adversity, as being yourselves also in the body.

Hebrews 13:3

Wherefore Jesus also, that he might sanctify the people with his own blood, suffered without the gate.

Let us go forth therefore unto him without the camp, bearing his reproach.

Hebrews 13:12,13

Of these things put *them* in remembrance, charging *them* before the Lord that they strive not about words to no profit, *but* to the subverting of the hearers.

II Timothy 2:14

Watch and pray, that ye enter not into temptation: the spirit indeed *is* willing, but the flesh *is* weak.

Matthew 26:41

Him that is weak in the faith receive ye, *but* not to doubtful disputations.

For one believeth that he may eat all things: another, who is weak, eateth herbs.

Let not him that eateth despise him that eateth not; and let not him which eateth not judge him that eateth: for God hath received him.

Romans 14:1-3

The night is far spent, the day is at hand: let us therefore cast off the works of darkness, and let us put on the armour of light.

Let us walk honestly, as in the day; not in rioting and drunkeness, not in chambering and wantonness, not in strife and envying.

But put ye on the Lord Jesus Christ, and make not provision for the flesh, to *fulfil* the lusts *thereof*.

Romans 13:12-14

Beloved, believe not every spirit, but try the spirits whether they are of God: because many false prophets are gone out into the world.

I John 4:1

And ye know that he was manifested to take away our sins; and in him is no sin.

Whosoever abideth in him sinneth not: whosoever sinneth hath not seen him, neither known him.

Little children, let no man deceive you: he that doeth righteousness is righteous, even as he is righteous.

He that committeth sin is of the devil; for the devil sinneth from the beginning. For this purpose the Son of God was manifested, that he might destroy the works of the devil.

I John 3:5-8

WE ARE COMMANDED TO CARE
FOR THOSE AROUND US BY...
Keeping Our Word

Therefore seeing we have this ministry, as we have received mercy, we faint not;

But have renounced the hidden things of dishonesty, not walking in craftiness, nor handling the word of God deceitfully; but by manifestation of the truth commending ourselves to every man's conscience in the sight of God.

II Corinthians 4:1,2

Wherefore putting away lying, speak every man truth with his neighbour: for we are members one of another.

Ephesians 4:25

Let no man deceive you with vain words: for because of these things cometh the wrath of God upon the children of disobedience.

Be not ye therefore partakers with them.

For ye were sometimes darkness, but now *are ye* light in the Lord: walk as children of light:

Ephesians 5:6-8

Now the things which I write unto you, behold, before God, I lie not.

Galatians 1:20

Lie not one to another, seeing that ye have put off the old man with his deeds;

Colossians 3:9

He that saith, I know him, and keepeth not his commandments, is a liar, and the truth is not in him.

But whoso keepeth his word, in him verily is the love of God perfected: hereby know we that we are in him.

He that saith he abideth in him ought himself also so to walk, even as he walked.

I John 2:4-6

Lord, who shall abide in thy tabernacle? who shall dwell in thy holy hill?

He that walketh uprightly, and worketh righteousness, and speaketh the truth in his heart.

He that backbiteth not with his tongue, nor doeth evil to his neighbour, nor taketh up a reproach against his neighbour.

Psalm 15:1-3

When thou vowest a vow unto God, defer not to pay it; for *he hath* no pleasure in fools: pay that which thou hast vowed.

Better *is it* that thou shouldest not vow, than that thou shouldest vow and not pay.

Ecclesiastes 5:4,5

Dare any of you, having a matter against another, go to law before the unjust, and not before the saints?

Do ye not know that the saints shall judge the world? and if the world shall be judged by you, are ye unworthy to judge the smallest matters?

Know ye not that we shall judge angels? how much more things that pertain to this life?

If then ye have judgments of things pertaining to this life, set them to judge who are least esteemed in the church.

I Corinthians 6:1-4

But above all things, my brethren, swear not, neither by heaven, neither by the earth, neither by any other oath: but let your yea be yea; and *your* nay, nay; lest ye fall into condemnation.

James 5:12

That no *man* go beyond and defraud his brother in *any* matter: because that the Lord *is* the avenger of all such, as we also have forewarned you and testified.

I Thessalonians 4:6

MY PRAYER LIST

MY PRAYER LIST

_____

_____

_____

_____

_____

_____

_____

_____

_____

_____

_____

_____

_____

_____

_____

_____

_____

_____

_____

_____

_____

_____

_____

_____

_____

_____

MY PRAYER LIST

_____
_____
_____
_____
_____
_____
_____
_____
_____
_____
_____
_____
_____
_____
_____
_____
_____
_____
_____
_____
_____
_____
_____
_____
_____
_____
_____
_____
_____

MY PRAYER LIST

_____

_____

_____

_____

_____

_____

_____

_____

_____

_____

_____

_____

_____

_____

_____

_____

_____

_____

_____

_____

_____

_____

_____

_____

_____

_____

_____

_____

MY PRAYER LIST

_____

_____

_____

_____

_____

_____

_____

_____

_____

_____

_____

_____

_____

_____

_____

_____

_____

_____

_____

_____

_____

_____

_____

_____

_____

_____

_____

_____

_____

MY PRAYER LIST

_____

_____

_____

_____

_____

_____

_____

_____

_____

_____

_____

_____

_____

_____

_____

_____

_____

_____

_____

_____

_____

_____

_____

_____

_____

_____

PERSONAL STUDY NOTES

PERSONAL STUDY NOTES

_____

_____

_____

_____

_____

_____

_____

_____

_____

_____

_____

_____

_____

_____

_____

_____

_____

_____

_____

_____

_____

_____

_____

_____

_____

_____

_____

_____

PERSONAL STUDY NOTES

Steps to Peace with God

Step 1 | God's Purpose: Peace and Life

God loves you and wants you to experience peace and life—abundant and eternal.

The Bible Says . . .

". . . we have peace with God through our Lord Jesus Christ." Romans 5:1

"For God so loved the world that He gave His only begotten Son, that whoever believes in Him should not perish but have everlasting life." John 3:16

". . . I have come that they may have life, and that they may have it more abundantly." John 10:10b

Since God planned for us to have peace and the abundant life right now, why are most people not having this experience?

Step 2 | Our Problem: Separation

God created us in His own image to have an abundant life. He did not make us as robots to automatically love and obey Him, but gave us a will and a freedom of choice.

We chose to disobey God and go our own willful way. We still make this choice today. This results in separation from God.

Our choice results in separation from God.

The Bible Says . . .

"For all have sinned and fall short of the glory of God." Romans 3:23

"For the wages of sin is death, but the gift of God is eternal life in Christ Jesus our Lord." Romans 6:23

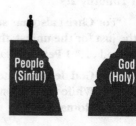

Our Attempts

Through the ages, individuals have tried in many ways to bridge this gap . . . without success . . .

The Bible Says . . .

"There is a way that seems right to man, but in the end it leads to death." Proverbs 14:12

"But your iniquities have separated you from God; and your sins have hidden His face from you, so that He will not hear." Isaiah 59:2

There is only c
remedy for this pı
lem of separation.

People (Sinful) Good Works Religion Philosophy Morality

Step 3 # God's Remedy: The Cross

Jesus Christ is the only answer to this problem. He died on the Cross and rose from the grave, paying the penalty for our sin and bridging the gap between God and people.

The Bible Says . . .

**". . . God is on one side and all the people on the other side, and Christ Jesus, Himself man, is between them to bring them together . . ."
1 Timothy 2:5**

"For Christ also has suffered once for sins, the just for the unjust, that He might bring us to God . . ." 1 Peter 3:18a

"But God demonstrates His own love for us in this: While we were still sinners, Christ died for us." Romans 5:8

God has provided t
only way . . . we m
make the choice . .

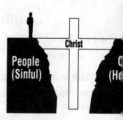

Christ

People (Sinful)

Step 4 | Our Response: Receive Christ

must trust Jesus Christ and receive Him by personal itation.

The Bible Says . . .

"Behold, I stand at the door and knock. If yone hears My voice and opens the door, I l come in to him and dine with him, and he h Me." Revelation 3:20

"But as many as received Him, to them He ve the right to become children of God, even those who believe in His name." John 1:12

". . . if you confess with your mouth the d Jesus and believe in your heart that God s raised Him from the dead, you will be saved." mans 10:9

Are you here . . . or here?

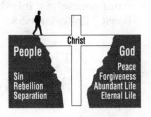

here any good reason why you cannot receive Jesus Christ right now?

How to receive Christ:

Admit your need (I am a sinner).

Be willing to turn from your sins (repent).

Believe that Jesus Christ died for you on the Cross and rose from the grave.

Through prayer, invite Jesus Christ to come in and control your life through the Holy Spirit. (Receive Him as Lord and Savior.)

What to Pray:

ar Lord Jesus,

I know that I am a sinner and need Your forgiveness. I believe that You d for my sins. I want to turn from my sins. I now invite You to come into heart and life. I want to trust and follow You as Lord and Savior.

In Jesus' name. Amen.

_____   _____
Date   Signature

God's Assurance: His Word

If you prayed this prayer,

The Bible Says...

"For 'whoever calls upon the name of the Lord will be saved.'" Romans 10:13

Did you sincerely ask Jesus Christ to come into your life? Where is He right now? What has He given you?

"For it is by grace you have been saved, through faith—and this is no[t] from yourselves, it is the gift of God—not by works, so that no one can boast." Ephesians 2:8,9

The Bible Says...

"He who has the Son has life; he who does not have the Son of God does not have life. These things I have written to you who believe in the name of the Son of God, that you may know that you have eternal life, and that you may continue to believe in the name of the Son of God." 1 John 5:12–13, NKJV

Receiving Christ, we are born into God's family through the supernatural work of the Holy Spirit who indwells every believer…this is called regeneration or the "new birth."

This is just the beginning of a wonderful new life in Christ. To deepen this relationship you should:

1. Read your Bible every day to know Christ better.
2. Talk to God in prayer every day.
3. Tell others about Christ.
4. Worship, fellowship, and serve with other Christians in a church where Christ is preached[.]
5. As Christ's representative in a needy world, demonstrate your new life by your love and concern for others.

God bless you as you do.

Billy Graham

If you want further help in the decision you have made, write to:
Billy Graham Evangelistic Association P.O. Box 779, Minneapolis, Minnesota 55440-0779